CHIN UP CHIN OUT JOB SEARCH

49 Ideas for Finding Work Faster & Easier

Shary Raske

Chin UP Chin OUT Job Search
49 Ideas for Finding Work Easier & Faster
Shary Raske
Buoyancy Publishing

Published by Buoyancy Publishing, St. Louis, MO
Copyright ©2018 Shary Raske
All rights reserved.

Editor: Lisbeth Tanz, FuzzyDogLLC.com
Illustrator: Katie Gounis
Cover and Interior design: Davis Creative, DavisCreative.com

Library of Congress Cataloging-in-Publication Data
Library of Congress Control Number: 2018904888

Shary Raske
Chin UP Chin OUT Job Search: 49 Ideas for Finding Work Easier & Faster
ISBN: 978-17320407-0-0
Library of Congress subject headings:
1. BUS037020 BUSINESS & ECONOMICS / Careers / Job Hunting
2. BUS056030 BUSINESS & ECONOMICS / Careers / Resumes
3. SEL024000 SELF-HELP / Self-Management / Stress Management

2018

ATTENTION CORPORATIONS, UNIVERSITIES, COLLEGES AND PROFESSIONAL ORGANIZATIONS: Quantity discounts are available on bulk purchases of this book for educational, gift purposes, or as premiums for increasing magazine subscriptions or renewals. Special books or book excerpts can also be created to fit specific needs. For information, please contact Buoyancy Publishing, shary@courageouschange.net

Table of Contents

To Karen Scheub

The first person to encourage me to keep writing!

Discouraged and Looking for Work? Your Courageous Change Begins Now.

This book is written for the thousands of job hunters who are down but not out and have a flickering hope that maybe, someday, they will be happy and working again. If that is you, read on. You will be getting ideas from me and from actual clients (names and circumstances changed to protect their identities). Your ideas are important, too.

There is no right or wrong way to read this book; you can read it all at once, or just read the summary of suggested actions at the end. Note that if the idea of God doesn't work for you, skip the Intentions section. Yet if you wish to bring a more spiritual approach into your search, it is there for you to use. You do not have to believe in God for this book to be beneficial. For me, prayer taps into some goodness that is greater than I am. "Amen" is like an affirmation and means, "May it Be So." It can strengthen your willingness to be in action.

In other words, you get to choose what is useful to you. Let go of the rest. You choose how this book will facilitate your Courageous Change. Experiment. Make mistakes. Try again. Keep going! You might even re-read a page of this book each day while you continue to job search. One small action each day can make a huge difference in your search.

Sometimes discouragement leads to despair, and despair leads to suicidal thoughts. I once worked with a professional who reached the conclusion that running into a bridge abutment was the best solution for not finding work. Never mind that he would be leaving behind two small children and a wife who loved him. This was not a viable solution. He had given up…at least temporarily. Happily, he did choose life and got the help he needed.

This book is not a substitution for psychotherapy. If you are thinking about ending your life…don't. You have other choices besides one that is so permanent. Really, you do. Call a mental health professional or dial a suicide hotline. You don't have to go through these feelings alone, nor do you have to act on them. Don't be embarrassed to call 911 if you are feeling that desperate.

All of us get discouraged. It is a part of the human experience. The key is not to stay there. If you are depressed and need to earn a living, it may still be possible to take a positive Action each day to find work. But it does require support and reaching out.

The hardest part of all is accepting that once you have asked for what you want, you may get a "No." Yet, without asking, you will never get a "Yes."

This book is intended to encourage, support, and guide.
Keep going until you hear those wonderful words: "Welcome aboard!"

Shary Raske
For additional Career Services contact me at www.CourageousChange.net

IDEA #1

GET OUT OF BED,
OR WILL EEYORE EVER CHANGE?

IDEA #1 GET OUT OF BED, OR WILL EEYORE EVER CHANGE?

What does a job search support group and the characters in Winnie the Pooh have in common? Pooh was a bear of little brain at the start of the story. Tigger bounced on people. Piglet was a very small animal, constantly afraid. Eeyore was despondent. Did any of them fundamentally change their personalities during each of their adventures? No! At the end of each story, Pooh was still a bear of little brain, Tigger was still bouncing, Piglet was still afraid, and Eeyore was still depressed. Yet somehow, because they had each other, whatever peril they were in was resolved. The same is true for a job search. If you start your search as a basically pessimistic person, chances are that when you find work you will still be a basically pessimistic person. The difference between finding work and not finding work is support. That's where job search support groups come in. Discouraged job hunters tend to isolate. Discouraged job hunters tend to tell the same sad stories. An honest, encouraging support group will guide you on how to tell a different story. Employers do not want to hear about your bad luck. They do not want to hear your sad story, even if it is a really good one. What they want from you is dedication, respect, and reassurance that you can do the job. Find people who can help you tell a better story. Better yet, find people who you can support, too.

INTENTION
Help me to accept my current situation exactly the way it is. Help me to know that it's okay to be me, whether I am Pooh, or Tigger, or Piglet, or Eeyore. Give me the energy to find a job search support group or a trusted friend that will be part of this career transition experience. Thank you, for your support. God, you are greater than my current situation. Amen!

ACTION
My promise today is to take one positive Action, even if it means just getting out of bed.

IDEA #1 GET OUT OF BED, OR WILL EEYORE EVER CHANGE?

My promise today is to take one positive Action, even if it means just getting out of bed.

What one positive Action will that be for you? Use the space below to handwrite what you will do today.

_____

_____

_____

_____

Writing your thoughts down is a physical act that gets into your body, not just in your head.
Write, draw, or scribble what one positive Action you will do today:

_____

_____

_____

_____

_____

IDEA #2

IF IT IS NOT DEPRESSION, COULD IT BE THAT YOU ARE GRIEVING?

IDEA #2 IF IT IS NOT DEPRESSION, COULD IT BE THAT YOU ARE GRIEVING?

There once was a man who jumped right in after he was laid off. He registered for employment at the State Career Center. He went to job search support groups, but nothing seemed to be happening. Initially it didn't seem to bother him. As time went on, he became immobilized.

When he asked himself, "What emotions am I feeling around my job search?" he had to admit he felt sadness and rage all bundled together. Truth was, he didn't want to work. He didn't want to get on with his life. Truth was he felt stuck until he admitted that he was grieving not only for the loss of his job, but also for all the other times in his life he didn't feel in control of his own destiny.

It may seem counter-intuitive to grieve in the middle of a job search. Actually grieving and really feeling the loss is an essential step BEFORE you can be effective in getting on with your job search. Maybe you think you have to keep pushing yourself. Maybe you think you must try to force solutions before you run out of cash. Grief knows no timelines. You may be fine one day and incapacitated the next. Grieving is like that.

If you are feeling stuck, ask yourself, "What is the source of my resistance? How big is my grieving?" Sometimes it's easier to feel stuck than to feel the deep pain of loss.

Loss seems to act like a magnet for all the other aspects of your life that didn't go the way you wanted. Maybe you never fully let go of the loss of a spouse or a parent or losing your favorite job.

If you are grieving, give yourself permission to feel the pain. You might think about creating a funeral-like ceremony to honor what you've been through. Buy a journal and write in it daily. Write down all the losses you have endured and survived. Write about the loss you are experiencing right now.

Letting go of your losses may free up some energy for your job search. By looking honestly at your situation, you may find a legacy of hope underneath all that pain, loss and frustration.

INTENTION
Comfort me when I do not feel in control of my own destiny. Help me grieve and let go of my losses. Amen!

ACTION
My promise today is to take one positive step to honor my losses. I will make a list of all my losses on different pieces of toilet paper. When it is time, I will flush this list down the toilet, and let my losses go.

IDEA #2 IF IT IS NOT DEPRESSION, COULD IT BE THAT YOU ARE GRIEVING?

My promise today is to take one positive step to honor my losses.
I will make a list of all my losses on different pieces of toilet paper.
When it is time, I will flush this list down the toilet, and let my losses go.

Sometimes doing something ridiculous like writing on toilet paper is a great way to get back into Action. Write or draw out your losses. Then take one positive Action, even it means flushing the toilet! Once you are out of bed, make it, too.

_____

_____

_____

_____

_____

_____

_____

IDEA #3

FORGIVE ME, WHAT WAS I DOING?
HOW TO OVERCOME A FUZZY BRAIN

IDEA #3 FORGIVE ME, WHAT WAS I DOING? HOW TO OVERCOME A FUZZY BRAIN

"Forgive me, sometimes I am fuzzy-headed, and the concept of time escapes me." What a gentle way to say that you are overwhelmed, scattered, and not functioning at optimal speed! We all have days like this. Sometimes we have weeks like this. Feeling stressed out and overwhelmed may happen a lot during a job search.

If you are depressed, you might feel intensely overwhelmed. If you are feeling fuzzy-headed, take a break. Pamper yourself by taking a relaxing bath. Light a candle. Listen to music. A spinning brain will keep you in circular thinking and only lead to more stress.

Think back to a time when you were so engaged in an activity that nothing else crept in. What's that for you? For some, it's cooking or cleaning or running errands. For others, it's dancing or washing the car or taking a brisk walk. Whatever that one thing is, do it now! Then, when the chatter slows down a bit, brainstorm 20 ways to take care of yourself. The list might look something like this:

    Dance to rock and roll music
    Hug a tree
    Take a walk
    Go to the library and check out a funny movie
    Play in the park
    Practice yoga (rent a video, check out one from
        the library, or watch YouTube)
    Take a pillow and pound on your bed until you're
        out of breath!

What is good self-care for you? It's easy to slip into destructive "self-care," like worshipping the refrigerator or the television for hours on end. That's why this list is important to create BEFORE you feel overwhelmed the next time. Tack your list on your refrigerator or some other prominent place like your bathroom mirror.

INTENTION

Thank you for reminding me that being overwhelmed is a normal part of change. Help me to remember to start each day with self-care first. Amen!

ACTION

My promise today is to do one thing from my self-care list, and then do one more. But first, I will get out of bed.

IDEA #3 FORGIVE ME, WHAT WAS I DOING? HOW TO OVERCOME A FUZZY BRAIN

My promise today is to do one thing from my self-care list, and then do one more.
But first, I will get out of bed.

How will you take care of yourself today?
Write about one Action that is fun or relaxing. Then do it!

_____

_____

_____

_____

_____

_____

_____

_____

_____

_____

_____

_____

_____

_____

_____

_____

_____

_____

_____

IDEA #4

WAYS TO GET MORE ENERGY

IDEA #4 WAYS TO GET MORE ENERGY

What were some things you did when you had energy? It's time to expand your self-care list. It might look like this:

1. Do 20 jumping jacks
2. March in place to John Phillips Sousa music
3. Go to the park and swing
4. Swim
5. Listen to Salsa music
6. Go to a coffee shop
7. Listen to a www.ted.com talk
8. Volunteer at your favorite charity
9. Help another person
10. Read funny books

Dig deep. Don't be surprised if you think this assignment seems ridiculous. Do it anyway. It may come as a surprise to you that having fun is essential to an effective job search, particularly if you are feeling down.

Once you have given yourself permission to create more energy, set up a 3 to 1 ratio. Do three fun things a day, then one job search activity. Do three more fun things, then one job search activity. That's right, three fun things first. After a week or when you feel your energy level coming back up, use a 2 to 1 ratio. Once you've gotten the hang of it, reverse the ratios: three job search activities to one fun activity. Take your time with this. Your goal is to create more energy.

INTENTION

Thank you for giving me permission to have fun, fun, fun, and then work...well at least in the short run. Thank you for giving me permission to relax as part of my job search plan. With your help, I'll keep taking Action and leaving the results to you. Amen!

ACTION

My promise is to experiment with doing THREE fun things today, then and only then, do ONE job search activity.

IDEA #4 WAYS TO GET MORE ENERGY

My promise is to experiment with doing THREE fun things today, then and only then, do ONE job search activity.

Write about how you will give yourself permission to relax and enjoy your day. What fun activities might you do? Then go do them!

_____

_____

_____

_____

_____

_____

_____

_____

_____

_____

_____

_____

IDEA #5

CREATE STRUCTURE AND GET ORGANIZED

IDEA #5 CREATE STRUCTURE AND GET ORGANIZED

Now it's time to take an inventory of how you spend your day. Write down all activities including the destructive ones like overeating, oversleeping, or watching 8 hours of television a day. Do not judge your list; just write it down. Record how much time you spend exercising, eating, resting, interacting with people, being alone, in leisure, and sleeping. Again, do not judge your list; just write it down. If you don't have a clue how you spend your day, then journal each hour of your day for five days. Then ask yourself, "How much time can I spend each week without exhausting myself?" Creating a Daily Action Plan will help you get out of the fog. Give yourself permission to start small: Day one, get dressed and get a cup of coffee. Return home and go to bed. A vital portion of your plan is to give yourself enough time to replenish.

Finding employment is like organizing a special project. Figure out how much time you can spend each week without wearing yourself out. It takes about a month to repeat your weekly plan before it becomes automatic. Until then, please be diligent to keep other activities from creeping into your plan. For instance, if you've been watching three hours of television each day and you want to use those three hours for job search activities, it will take a while to get out of the watching-too-much-television habit. It's helpful to leave the house or leave the room that the television is in.

There is no right or wrong plan. A plan that commits to doing three things a day is just as valid as a plan that measures activity by the number of hours worked. The key is your plan must work for you. Consistency is also vital. Once you've started, don't stop. If you take a week off, it's been my experience that it takes three weeks to build back up the momentum you previously had. If you'd like to read about how to measure forward progress, read IDEA #43. The rest of the book will teach you how to build up to that.

INTENTION

Help me to remember that "GOD" stands for Good Orderly Direction. Give me the strength to do the next right thing. Help me to put one foot in front of the other, each day and every day. Help me to organize my day so it is filled with life and productivity and fun. Thank you for giving me a mind that works, at least some of the time. Amen!

ACTION

My promise today is to pay attention to how I spend my time, and let go of the activities that just numb me out.

IDEA #5 CREATE STRUCTURE AND GET ORGANIZED

My promise today is to pay attention to how I spend my time, and let go of the activities that just numb me out.

Draw a picture of putting one foot in front of the other.
Draw a picture of a clock.
Write about where you spend your time.

_____

_____

_____

_____

_____

IDEA #6

STAY AWAY FROM INEFFECTIVE ACTIVITIES THAT DEPLETE YOU

IDEA #6 STAY AWAY FROM INEFFECTIVE ACTIVITIES THAT DEPLETE YOU

Are you starting your day going online to job search boards and applying for work? Are you spending more than 4 hours a day searching for work online? Stop! Never apply for jobs online at the beginning of the day. Instead, wait until 3:00 p.m. and then spend no more than 90 minutes a day online.

Stop activities where you submit a resume and never hear back. It will just make you more despondent. Besides, if you are currently putting 100% of your job search efforts in less than 18% of the available job openings, you may eventually find work, but at what psychological and financial cost?

If you are really depressed, do not go to job search boards at all for at least four weeks, or until you have a better plan in place. Unless you are applying for accounting, information technology, or administrative assistant positions, only 10-18% of all job openings are found through job search boards. If you are really depressed, do not go to job fairs as these typically yield a poor return on identifying any job openings.

Let me make it very clear: spend less than 25% of your total search plan applying for jobs online, applying for jobs through a company website, applying for jobs by going to job fairs, or thinking a recruiter might help.

You might balk at this notion. For some of you, this is all you have ever known to do. You might think that some activity is better than no activity.

I would agree IF you are getting results. If you are not getting results, then stay away from ineffective activities that deplete you. Go get a cup of coffee instead.

You will be learning how to fill the other 75% of your job search time. For now, do not apply for work online until after 3:00 p.m.

Eventually, you will develop a consistent action plan that includes what you want to do, an evaluation of what happened, support, and learning. Remember it takes about a month to build new habits.

INTENTION
Give me the willingness to be open to new ways of job searching. Guide my actions so my energy will be restored. Give me the courage to write a Daily Action Plan and then do it. Amen!

ACTION
My promise is to wait to apply for jobs online until after 3:00 p.m. My promise is to get out of bed, get dressed as if I were going to work, and then leave the house, even if it means driving around the block and coming back home.

IDEA #6 STAY AWAY FROM INEFFECTIVE ACTIVITIES THAT DEPLETE YOU

My promise is to wait to apply for jobs online until after 3:00 p.m. My promise is to get out of bed, get dressed as if I were going to work, and then leave the house, even if it means driving around the block and coming back home.

Draw a picture of you applying for jobs online, and then draw a line through it. How would you spend that extra time if you didn't apply for jobs online, at least for today? Write about what that would be like for you.

_____

_____

_____

_____

_____

IDEA #7

STOP! STAY AWAY FROM PEOPLE WHO DEPLETE YOU

IDEA #7 STOP! STAY AWAY FROM PEOPLE WHO DEPLETE YOU

Every job search support group has one person in it who wants to bring you down. Don't try to fix or encourage that person, just stay away. Every job search support group has one person in it who isn't really looking for a job, but just wants a place to occupy their time. Don't try to fix or encourage that person either. When you are depressed, you may end up being like a magnet attracting other depressed people, particularly in a job search support group. If you find yourself talking to someone who is depleting you quickly, and I mean quickly, excuse yourself and find someone else to talk to. It might sound something like this, "Excuse me, I apologize for interrupting, but there are a couple of other people I'd like to talk to before the program starts. Thanks for understanding." Then walk away.

There once was a woman who couldn't help herself. She became immobilized due to listening to negative people who told her she was too old to find a job, she wouldn't find work because she didn't have a college degree, and she would be discriminated against because it was a male-dominated world. I urged her to stop interacting with them, period. For her, that meant not going to any job search support groups. Within 8 weeks, she had landed work that paid her more money, provided her greater satisfaction, and offered her a great career path.

The truth is that other people cannot predict what will happen to you. They are just guessing. So if you are going to make something up in your head, wouldn't be better to make up something that has a positive outcome? I can't predict how quickly you will find work. The point of the story is being around negative energy is not good for you and will slow you down.

What if the people who deplete you are your loved ones? What if you have a rebellious son who says you are a loser? What if you have a partner who says you are lazy and no good? What if you have had a history of allowing this kind of verbal abuse? Walk away from people who deplete you. It may mean therapy, leaving the house more frequently, or learning how to be assertive in a firm, but gentle way. One person I know created an imaginary shield that protected him from the inevitable onslaught of negative feedback. Do not argue, justify, or escalate. Just walk away. Your job is not to fix them, but to focus on getting back on your feet, and learning how to be a better job searcher.

INTENTION
Protect me from negative people. Guide my actions so that my energy will be restored. Give me the courage to stay away from people who deplete me. Amen!

ACTION
I promise to make a plan to protect myself from negative people. My promise is to get out of bed, get dressed, leave the house, and start looking for positive people.

IDEA #7 STOP! STAY AWAY FROM PEOPLE WHO DEPLETE YOU

I promise to make a plan to protect myself from negative people. My promise is to get out of bed, get dressed, leave the house, and start looking for positive people.

Draw a picture of you staying away from negative people.

Where are the positive people?
In a bowling alley? Coffee shop? In church? Hiking at a park?
Start looking and smile while you look!

IDEA #8

FIXING TO GET READY TO

IDEA #8 FIXING TO GET READY TO

When I lived in Oklahoma, there was an expression that I just loved, "I'm fixing to get ready to." Are you fixing to get ready to conduct an effective job search? We've discussed how to get mentally ready. Now it's time to discuss how to get physically ready. Where is the best place for your job search headquarters? Some set up it up in their basement (not recommended). For others, it's the dining room table. For others, their headquarters is at the library. If you are lucky enough, there may be a spare bedroom available. You want a place that is just for search activities, not paying the bills, not helping the kids with their homework. You want a place that when you sit down, you are ready for business.

How do you organize yourself? Some use folders. Some use three-ring notebooks with subject tabs. Some people use a contact management database to keep track of information, and to remind them about upcoming appointments. Some have a planner that they carry with them at all times. What works best for you to easily retrieve historical information? Again, there is no right or wrong. For those who like to make piles of paper, don't stop! What matters is that you can find information easily.

Do you have a computer and printer? If not, where can you go to borrow someone else's computer? Do you have access to the internet? If not, the public library will let you access the internet an hour at a time. "Fixing to get ready to" means taking inventory of what you need to have a successful search. Phone? Check. Resume? Check. Business cards? Check.

Bring colors, textures, and sounds to your workspace. Soon, we will be focusing on creating a career transition plan that includes occupations you are targeting, organizations you want to learn more about, and your compelling message. We'll be fixing to get ready to figure that out, too!

INTENTION

If I build it, will they come? Help me to create a place just for my job search to take myself seriously. Guide my preparations so that when I sit down to go to work, I'm ready. Thank you for giving me the willingness to get ready. Amen!

ACTION

My promise today is to breathe and relax as I create my inspiring job search headquarters.

IDEA #8 FIXING TO GET READY TO

My promise today is to breathe and relax as I create my inspiring job search headquarters.

What textures, light, and colors will you bring into your job search headquarters?
What sounds will you bring into your job search headquarters?

_____

_____

_____

_____

_____

_____

_____

Write below all the elements of your ideal workspace:

_____

_____

_____

_____

_____

_____

_____

_____

_____

_____

_____

_____

_____

_____

_____

IDEA #9

MAKE SOME MISTAKES, BUT TAKE ACTION ANYWAY

IDEA #9 MAKE SOME MISTAKES, BUT TAKE ACTION ANYWAY

When you take Action, plan ahead of time that you will not always get the result you want. In fact, you may make a mistake or fail to enlist an important person into your cause. Plan ahead of time that you will bounce back. Plan ahead of time that you will have opportunities to forgive yourself and opportunities to forgive others. The time for hiding is over. You will make mistakes. The key is to bounce back.

The tricky part is learning how to manage the fear, the panic and the self-loathing long enough to do ONE thing toward your job search. Remember, depression is a liar. If you listen to the part of you that is depressed, you might conclude you have nothing to offer, particularly if you have abused yourself with months and months of applying for jobs online and have nothing to show for it. It isn't you. You just need a better strategy. You may have forgotten your greatness, but you can take slow and steady steps to get your confidence back. Here are the basic PREPARATION steps to getting back to work:

1. Develop strategies for emotional self-care.
2. Take stock of your current skills, interests, and what is important to you.
3. Evaluate what part of your work history you enjoyed. Give yourself permission to attract it again.
4. Evaluate what part of your work history was abusive, depressing, or never quite right for you. Later, during job interviews, you will ask good questions. Be very alert, and listen to your gut so you don't attract a bad job again.

5. Take stock of your aptitudes and activities you do effortlessly.
6. Learn what kinds of occupations would express your skills, interests, and values.
7. Rehearse ways to talk about yourself from a place of power. Memorize the positive things you will say and include your ideas of what kind of occupations you will explore. Build on the good.
8. Develop ways to overcome any perceived liabilities you might have. These include being out of work longer than a year, job-hopping, age, gender, race, religion, chronic illness, or hospitalizations. Each perceived liability needs a compensatory strategy to prevent it from being a barrier to getting the job you want.

Remember that you don't have to do all 8 steps in a single day. Map out what works for you.

INTENTION
Guide my actions so that my confidence will be restored. Give me the courage to look inside and find the good. Help me to get ready to take stock of my life. Amen!

ACTION
I promise to read an inspiring book or watch an inspiring movie where the hero comes from behind and wins. My promise is to make mistakes and try again.

IDEA #9 MAKE SOME MISTAKES, BUT TAKE ACTION ANYWAY

I promise to read an inspiring book or watch an inspiring movie where the hero comes from behind and wins. My promise is to make mistakes and try again.

Mistakes come in many shapes and sizes.
Draw a shape (a mud puddle, lightning bolt, triangle, or some other shape).

Add your best guess of mistakes you will make.
Then draw a fence around them and keep them contained.
Keep going, even when you make mistakes.

IDEA #10

THE BASICS: LET OTHERS KNOW WHO YOU ARE

IDEA #10 THE BASICS: LET OTHERS KNOW WHO YOU ARE

Right now, you are the best kept secret in the world. You have a bundle of talent with a willingness to work and no one knows about it. Even though others have similar skills, your execution of those skills is unique to you. What do you value? What is important to you? This is the time to tell your story in a powerful way to enlist others to help. There are things you say, and things you don't say.

First, give a brief summary of your background. Here's an example: *For the past 12 years, I have had two different careers: one was in non-profit fundraising and the other one in selling tangible goods. What I enjoy about my work is learning the goals of my organization and then making those goals a reality. I get results by listening carefully to others, asking the right questions, and offering solutions that work.* OR

I am looking for work as an accountant because I enjoy the pursuit of accuracy! When I balance the books to the penny, it gives my employer detailed information on how to make better decisions.

Your summary should be brief and to the point. How would you summarize your background? Do not list everything you've done; only showcase what is consistent with what you want to do in the future. Then give an example that begins: What I enjoy about my work is.... If you feel resistance, try to remember when you did enjoy your work, and talk about that. Be positive.

Do not give ANY information that is not consistent with attracting your positive future. Do not say:
- You have been despondent and inactive.
- You have been out of work way too long.
- Your previous boss was abusive.

Finally, stop telling your sad story. Put this information in your journal instead.

Practice your presentation with people you know who will not shame or discourage you. If you don't have anyone safe, then practice talking in front of a mirror. Practice, practice, practice, and then practice some more. Now do something silly like standing on your head or saying "Ho, Ho, Ha, Ha, Ha, Ho, Ho, Ha, Ha, He." Now practice again. This time, smile when you talk about what you enjoy.

INTENTION
Thank you for giving me the words that tell my story. Give me the courage to start telling my positive story to others who can help me. Amen!

ACTION
Today I promise to prepare a summary of the positive aspects of who I am and what I enjoy doing. Then I promise to rehearse my powerful story until it becomes second nature to me.

IDEA #10 THE BASICS: LET OTHERS KNOW WHO YOU ARE

Today I promise to prepare a summary of the positive aspects of who I am and what I enjoy doing. Then I promise to rehearse my powerful story until it becomes second nature to me.

Fill in the blanks:
FOR CHANGING CAREERS – For the past ___ years, I have been working as a _____. What I enjoy about my work is _____, _____, and _____. I am at a point in my career where I would like to change careers into _____. Here's why: _____
Who do you know with experience in this field?

OR…

FOR STAYING IN SIMILAR WORK – For the past ___ years, I have been working as a _____. What I enjoy about my work is _____, _____, and _____. I would like to continue to learn more about how to _____ and make the best contribution I can at my next job. Who do you know that I could talk to get firsthand information about this?

(Helpful Hint: Do you prefer working with things, people, or ideas? I'll be asking you to take an inventory of your preferred interests and skills. Be thinking about that now as you create a summary of your positive aspects of yourself.)

IDEA #11

DON'T DO IT ALONE

IDEA #11 DON'T DO IT ALONE

It's ironic. The very person you think you should turn to for support probably isn't the best person to ask. Why? Because there is a built-in conflict of interest. If you are financially tied to your loved one, then he or she will need support, too. If it's Dad or Mom or a sibling, they have a certain image of you that may or may not help you discern your options. The other conflict of interest is your loved ones will worry. You have enough of that as it is.

Don't get me wrong, loved ones often ARE there for you; but their support is limited. Better to get an impartial team built around you. Choose people who are not tied financially to you. Choose people who have been through a successful search within the last three years. Choose people who are gentle and respectful when they give you feedback that you are missing the mark.

I recommend you find a positive person(s) for your team. You will need:

A Taskmaster. The role of the taskmaster is to go over your weekly plan. At the end of the week, the taskmaster will say, "Did you keep your promises? If not, what got in the way? What is your plan for next week?" Note that none of these questions is shaming or demeaning. These questions are for accountability.

An Encourager. Most people do not get through a search without feeling panic, anger, and feeling down. And it will happen more than once. An Encourager allows you to intentionally retreat and be comforted, but also encourages you to get back in the game. Note that an Encourager doesn't rescue or feel sorry for you.

A Cheerleader. When you are feeling wounded, the cheerleader is there to remind you of your greatness. The cheerleader reminds you are a good person, that you have a lot to offer, and that your future employer will be lucky to have you.

A Reality Check Guide. Let's say you are looking for an accounting job but find yourself applying for a dog food sales rep position. Your Reality Check Guide will gently remind you to get back on track. However, IF being a dog food sales rep is truly more appealing than being an accountant, use Career Research meetings to determine HOW to make this move. Resist the urge to simply apply online. Don't allow others to talk you into a job that isn't right for you, and don't do it to yourself either. The Realty Check Guide will ask, "Help me understand how this occupation fits with your overall interests and skills."

INTENTION

Help me to not overuse my loved ones for venting and complaining. Thank you for bringing people into my life who will be part of my success team. I will go home at night with my head held high, and really be there for my loved ones. Amen!

ACTION

My promise today is to reach out to others to encourage me and hold me accountable.

IDEA #11 DON'T DO IT ALONE

My promise today is to reach out to others to encourage me and hold me accountable.

What kind of positive people do you want on your volunteer job search team? Cut out pictures from magazines or find images online, or use actual photographs of people you know. Paste positive images of your future team on this page. Then be OPEN, receptive, and willing to search for actual people. Let the hunt begin!

IDEA #12

TRAIN YOUR LOVED ONES AND FRIENDS

IDEA #12 TRAIN YOUR LOVED ONES AND FRIENDS

It's well-meaning but so demoralizing! You know the dreaded: "You got a job, yet?" Typically, this comes from good friends or a family member. They mean well. They want to help, but they don't know how. That's where you come in. You have to train them NOT to ask this question. You must also train them NOT to ask, "Why haven't you got a job, yet?"

Instead, train them to ask you if you are keeping your commitments. Train them to ask:

"How can I support you?"
"Do you need someone to scream and whine and wail with you?"

And then train them to set limits with you.

Sometimes it's not easy being around someone who is depressed and looking for work. While you want them to be there for you, you don't want to exhaust them either. Well, maybe a little. Who doesn't like to tell a good traumatic story? Tell your friends and loved ones, "Look, I know I've been down, and I want to use you as a sounding board. Yet I am also aware of being really needy right now. My fear is if I reach out to you too often, you will go away and not want to be with me anymore. So what will work for you? Is it okay to complain and be down with you for ten minutes a day? Once a week for a half an hour? What works for you?" Tell them that they have permission to say, "I can't talk right now, could we touch base tomorrow?" Then ask permission to remind them NOT to ask the "You got a job, yet?" question.

You are creating mutual support. Your job search will affect others, too. You want to be able to ask for what you need, and understand what they need, too.

INTENTION

Thank you, God for the opportunity to have mutual support in my life. I know I've been isolating and staying away from well-meaning friends. Help me to reach out to them and ask them for support. Help me to write a letter to the ones I've driven away and let them know that I am sorry. Let me write and request what I need if I don't have the energy to verbally ask. Protect me and comfort me if they don't respond the way I want. Amen!

ACTION

My promise today is to train my loved ones to only ask me if I am keeping my promises. I will reassure them that I have a plan and am moving forward.

IDEA #12 TRAIN YOUR LOVED ONES AND FRIENDS

My promise today is to train my loved ones to only ask me if I am keeping my promises. I will reassure them that I have a plan and am moving forward.

Find a picture of a shield and paste is here (or draw one yourself).

What is your self-protection strategy if you request support from a friend or loved one and they say, "No?" How will you take a stand for yourself if a friend or loved one doesn't want to help?

_____

_____

_____

_____

IDEA #13

LET'S GET STARTED

IDEA #13 LET'S GET STARTED

Okay, you have your support team in place, you've trained your loved ones, and you've created your job search headquarters. Now it's time to get to work. Your plan is simple. Each day you will answer these questions:

1. Who do I want to see?
2. What do I want to say?
3. When am I going to budget the time to take an action?
4. Who will hold me accountable to my action plan?

You will need to know what your occupational focus is, what organizations you want as potential employers, and how to generate introductions into those organizations. This is the time to be reading books about how to conduct informational meetings, how to job interview, how to salary negotiate, and how to create visibility, even if you don't feel like it.

If you don't have an occupational focus, trust that you will develop one. If you don't know how to build a list of potential organizations, trust that you will learn. Be careful to do this slowly so you can integrate the concepts without getting overwhelmed. I'd rather you work 45 minutes a day consistently than get exhausted emotionally by doing too much. There is much to learn. Be gentle with yourself.

If you think all you have to do is write a great resume and cover letter and then apply for jobs online, think again. You want a comprehensive plan and applying online is only a small part of it. In fact, online job openings average only 18% for most op-portunities and applying for jobs online is a great way to keep hiding. Your plan needs to be bigger and more diverse for you to get you where you want to be.

Take a deep breath.

It may seem impossible at first to expand your plan to other, more effective job search activities. Your initial target is for you to eventually work up to a 5-hour workday. If you are spending more than 3 hours a day going online at job posting sites, stop now. What is 18% of a 5-hour workday? That's less than an hour a day. I recommend for you to stop applying online until you have your plan in place, and then no more than 45 minutes a day, after 3:00 p.m. once your plan is in place. Use the extra time you just created to replenish, be more organized, and learn other job search methods. Again, take a deep breath. It's time to get to work. When you eventually achieve a longer workday, then give yourself permission to be online up to 90 minutes a day.

INTENTION
Thank you for giving me hope that I can take action even if I am still discouraged. Thank you for giving me permission to take it slowly. Guide my actions today and give me a willingness to change. Amen!

ACTION
I promise to utilize time as a resource to get my job search plan in place.

IDEA #13 LET'S GET STARTED

I promise to utilize time as a resource to get my job search plan in place.

Draw a picture of a mountain; then draw a picture of you half way up. Congratulations, you are on your way!

IDEA #14

WHEN YOU ARE STRESSED OUT, THINK ABOUT FUN JOBS

IDEA #14 WHEN YOU ARE STRESSED OUT, THINK ABOUT FUN JOBS

We all have bad days. On those days, you might want to imagine doing work that looks like fun, or at least easy. What's that for you? For some, working as a bicycle mechanic would be fun; for others, being an over-the-road truck driver; for still others, it might be selling flowers in a grocery store. Whatever you imagine, there's always a reason why you picked your "easy" job. It is usually because there are parts to the job where you know you would excel. You want to feel competent again. You may have more skills to reach for a higher paying job, but for now give yourself permission to think about anything you want.

Think again about those fun job options.
 What abilities would you be using?
 What values would you be expressing?
 What makes this job idea appealing?

Hold on to those thoughts, because whatever that is for you, it's important. Fill in the blank: I want a job where I am_____. You might say, "I want a job where I am appreciated" or "I want a job where I'm left alone" or "I want a job where I travel" or "I want a job where I fix things." What is that for you? Honor your answers. It is important. Write them down.

A job search is anything but easy. Once you create the structure that mimics what a job had pro-

vided for you, it does get better. Figure out when to get up, what job search activities you will do, how much is too much, how much is too little, and when to stop. Let's face it, it can be a pain, but once the structure is in place, it becomes easier. You know what you will be doing on Monday. You know what you will be doing on Tuesday. Eventually the schedule will become second nature to you, and your job search will no longer be hard.

But first, practice saying out loud what you want.

INTENTION
God, I want to dream about fun jobs. Help me to relax as I create structure for my job search. Help me to rest when I need to rest and take action when I need to take action. Help me to trust that once my job search routine is established that I will feel more competent again. In the meantime, thank you for giving me permission to dream. Amen!

ACTION
My promise today is to pay attention to possible dream jobs. I promise to write down and acknowledge that inside those ideas are important clues about what I want to do.

IDEA #14 WHEN YOU ARE STRESSED OUT, THINK ABOUT FUN JOBS

My promise today is to pay attention to possible dream jobs. I promise to write down and acknowledge that inside those ideas are important clues about what I want to do.

Fill in the blank:

I want a job where I am_____

I want a job where I am_____

I want a job where I am_____

I want a job where I am_____

I want a job where I am_____

I want a job where I am_____

I want a job where I am_____

I want a job where I am_____

I want a job where I am_____

I want a job where I am_____

I want a job where I am_____

(Repeat ten or more times. There are no right or wrong answers. Just give yourself permission to say what you want.)

I want a job where I am_____

I want a job where I am_____

I want a job where I am_____

I want a job where I am_____

I want a job where I am_____

I want a job where I am_____

I want a job where I am_____

I want a job where I am_____

I want a job where I am_____

I want a job where I am_____

I want a job where I am_____

IDEA #15

THE BASICS: WHAT OCCUPATIONS ARE YOU TARGETING?

IDEA #15 THE BASICS: WHAT OCCUPATIONS ARE YOU TARGETING?

This is an opportunity to reinvent yourself, to attract something better. One of the basics of an excellent job search is to come up with three occupations you are targeting: A primary, a secondary, and a backup. Yes, you have options, even in a difficult job market, and even if you have a few strikes against you. This is a good time to learn about other options.

Choosing the right occupation may take several weeks of introspection and research, particularly if you didn't like what you have done in the past. Make your best guess. Don't worry. I will teach you how to do career research meetings to validate if you are on the right track.

In the meantime, focus on what skills do you want to use and those you never want to be caught using again. That's right, you get to choose! This is your life and you have options. What do you enjoy doing?

Be honest about how you made your previous occupational choices. Were those choices someone else's idea and you took the path of least resistance? Were these choices your idea or your parents'? Were your occupational choices a form of punishment because you didn't think you deserved anything better? If you answered "yes" to any of these questions, can you see why job searching would seem so dreadful to you? Why would you choose the very occupations that were so lifeless for you? There is hope. People do stumble into work without any forethought and it's perfect for them. But you are more likely to find what is right for you with forethought.

Sometimes people stay in occupations that are no longer economically viable. If you have been a dishwasher all your life and suddenly everyone starts using paper plates, no matter how good of a dishwasher you are, there won't be any job openings, through no fault of your own. Adapting to change is never easy, but if this is your situation, it's time to get retrained or retooled into something different. This is your chance to attract something better. Many community colleges and other job-related non-profits offer assessment and retooling programs. Search for them now.

Get thyself to the library to learn more about occupational options or go to www.bls.gov (Bureau of Labor and Statistics) and choose the link that says, "Occupational Outlook Handbook." Currently, this is under a link called "Career Information." Since web pages are often updated; if it's not there, keep looking!

INTENTION
Help me to be willing to believe that there is something better for me occupationally. Help me to trust that answers will come, even when I doubt. Thank you for giving me the energy to learn more about what occupations would be a better fit. Amen!

ACTION
My promise today is to learn more about what occupations might be a good fit for me. I promise to be open to a better life and explore occupations that work for me.

IDEA #15 THE BASICS: WHAT OCCUPATIONS ARE YOU TARGETING?

My promise today is to learn more about what occupations might be a good fit for me. I promise to be open to a better life and explore occupations that work for me.

IDEA #16

TAKE A STEP BACK AND BREATHE!

IDEA #16 TAKE A STEP BACK AND BREATHE!

By now you have probably figured out that if you are going to be successful at any job search project, it will require two things: radical self-care and taking responsibility for your actions. Radical self-care means being gentle with yourself and others. Radical self-care means going back to IDEAS #3 and #4 and doing them daily, or sometimes hourly. Radical self-care means creating positive support from others, even if that means just driving to a coffee shop (yes you can go in, even if you don't buy anything). Radical self-care means journaling about your fears, what overwhelms you, your procrastination, your resentments, your bitterness, or your sorrows. Your emotions are your emotions. Do not judge them or think you shouldn't be feeling these things. If you keep pushing those feelings down without acknowledging them, chances are your energy level will revert back to sludge. Your feelings are just features of being human.

You will be reading several more IDEAS that outline a Basic Job Search. You have my permission to read them and not necessarily act on them just yet. Chances are you will do battle with the part of you that feels inadequate. Chances are there will be a part of you that says, "It's too late" or "These ideas might work for others, but they won't work for me." And you may be right. Yet even then, you have options to start over or find something that will work for you.

You may even choose to repeat IDEAS #1 through 9 for a few weeks, or stop altogether and strategically retreat. There is no right or wrong way to how quickly you approach an effective job search. You will make mistakes, and that is okay. You get to choose whether you have had enough of the old way or not. Remember, depression is a liar. You do have options. You deserve the support needed to move forward.

As I said earlier, an effective job search requires two things: radical self-care and taking responsibility for your positive actions. If you make one promise each day and actually do it, (even if it is making your bed or walking outside) check in after ten days and see if you feel better. Until then, step back and breathe!

INTENTION
Guide my steps today. Give me courage to journal, to walk, and to learn other ways to job search. Thank you for giving me options for focusing on radical self-care. Amen!

ACTION
My promise today is to face my fears and let them pass through. I promise to relax as I learn new things.

IDEA #16 TAKE A STEP BACK AND BREATHE!

My promise today is to face my fears and let them pass through. I promise to relax as I learn new things.

Today my Radical Self-Care Plan will be:

_____

_____

_____

_____

Today I will take responsibility for my job search by:

_____

_____

_____

_____

After I have taken Action in doing both my self-care plan and my job search actions, I will reward myself by:

_____

_____

_____

_____

IDEA #17

THE BASICS: CHOOSE TARGET MARKETS

IDEA #17 THE BASICS: CHOOSE TARGET MARKETS

Target markets are things such as advertising, banking, or biotechnology companies. There are more markets, a lot more. There is a saying, "If you don't know where you are going, chances are you'll end up somewhere else." Let's say you have a few occupations in mind. Do you really need to know what markets you will be targeting? If you are an accountant or an IT professional, the answer is "maybe." For everyone else, the answer is "yes." Industry experience (or lack thereof), does count. If you are changing industries, you need to learn how to bridge the lack-of-experience gap.

Here is where I get the most resistance. Many of my clients protest and say, "But I don't want to limit my options." I beg to disagree. Less is actually more. Here's why: Let's say you live in a community that has 10,000 employers with revenues of more than $20,000,000 a year. Each one of those employers currently has occupational choices similar to what you are targeting. Wouldn't you agree that it would be physically impossible to approach them all?

"Well," they protest. "We'll only apply for jobs that are advertised." That might work well if it weren't for the fact that you are dumping yourself into a pool of applicants that could range from 100 to 500 people for the same job. What are your chances that you will be picked? There is another way: narrow your options.

One way to filter your options is to screen them by what is interesting to you. Make a list of what is personally appealing. Your list might be as diverse as this example: Cooking, Reading, Home Remodeling, Landscaping, Investing, Sports. Did you know that each of your interests has parallel organizations? Do you want to work for a non-profit organization or a profit-making organization? Do you identify more with tangible products or intangible services? You get to choose! This is the beginning of a pro-active search, instead of just reacting to what is advertised. You still have many choices that won't be as overwhelming as choosing everything.

INTENTION

Thank you for giving me a brain that works even when I am feeling pessimistic. Give me the patience to figure this out; trusting that if I do this step, my job search will be shortened. Thinking about industries and market sectors that match up to my interests is new to me. Help me accept the challenge to think about both my limits and my potential. Amen!

ACTION

My promise today is to make a list of 20 things that personally interest me (or used to interest me). I will choose my top five to match similar industries and markets.

IDEA #17 THE BASICS: CHOOSE TARGET MARKETS

My promise today is to make a list of 20 things that personally interest me (or used to interest me). I will choose my top five to match similar industries and markets.

What non-profits do you admire? What causes would you support?

_____

_____

_____

If you went into a bookstore, what topics would interest you? What are you curious about?

_____

_____

_____

Rank these types of organizations in the order that interests you. Cross out the ones that don't interest you.

_____ Transportation / Logistics
_____ Building Things / Construction
_____ Working in the Trades: Electrical, Plumbing, Insulation, Windows, Heating and Cooling
_____ Agriculture / Farming / Lawn and Garden / Flowers
_____ Making things / Manufacturing
_____ Processing Transactions / Banking / Insurance / Financial Services
_____ Helping others: Healthcare, Customer Service, Training, Home Services, Non-profits
_____ Consumer Goods / Retail
_____ Professional Services, Consulting, Legal, Counseling, Accounting, Engineering
       Information Technology, Computers, eCommerce
_____ Feeding People, Entertaining People
_____ New Business Launches / Innovative Products / Generating Better Ideas
_____ Public Service / Government
_____ Schools, Universities
_____ Communication Services / Writing / Marketing / Social media / Media / Phones / Radio
_____ Other: please list:

IDEA #18

THE BASICS: DEVELOP A JOB SEARCH FOCUS OR AT LEAST YOUR BEST GUESS

IDEA #18 THE BASICS:
DEVELOP A JOB SEARCH FOCUS OR AT LEAST YOUR BEST GUESS

Okay, you've inventoried what industries and/or market sectors you want to target. Now it is time to research industries by SIC and NAICS codes. These codes help you understand the different ways that business and organizational databases are categorized. There's a code for banks, a code for advertising, a code for coffee shops. There are thousands of codes, yet in the SIC system there are only ten larger categories. They are 1) Agriculture, Forestry, Fishing; 2) Mining; 3) Construction; 4) Manufacturing; 5) Transportation and Public Utilities; 6) Wholesale Trade; 7) Retail Trade; 8) Finance, Insurance, and Real Estate; 9) Services; and 10) Public Administration.

This is the time to learn about business and organizational databases. Most libraries have them. Check with your reference librarian if you need guidance. Ask: "How can I research companies by SIC or NAICS codes?" (You can get the same information by using NAICS codes. It's just a different system.) To locate just the codes (and not the corresponding organizations), go to: http://www.naics.com/search.htm. Keep in mind that the SIC is an older, simpler classification system. Choose one or the other. Both will get you the information you need.

If this step is overwhelming, be gentle and set a pace that works for you. Sometimes going to a bookstore and allowing yourself to gravitate toward a particular topic might be easier. If you can still find a hard copy of a Yellow Pages telephone book (the library might have one), try flipping through the Yellow Pages. Write down what classifications appeal to you. These are important clues. What topics do you randomly find appealing in the Yellow Pages? Write them down. Flip back and forth several times. Write down topics, even if they don't make sense to you.

Slowly but surely, you will build both an occupational focus and a list of actual organizations that may end up being potential employers. You want no more than three occupations, four primary markets, and then 30 to 100 names of organizations within those four markets. Another way to get ideas is to drive around town and get curious. As you travel ask: "I wonder what kind of businesses are in that office building?" Or, "I wonder how many businesses are involved in building a skyscraper?" Or, "What kind of charities are in my community?"

Get a bunch of ideas, and then whittle them down later to have fewer options. Set priorities. What is the most appealing to you? Be gentle as you explore. Give yourself permission to be both hopeful and a little nervous.

INTENTION
Thank you for giving me a mind to think and a mind to choose. Remind me that I have options, even when my negative thinking tells me I don't. With your help, I will act as if this preparation will get my job search going in the right direction. Amen!

ACTION
Today, I promise to go to a bookstore to see how topics are organized. I promise to go to the library and learn how organizations are classified.

IDEA #18 THE BASICS: DEVELOP A JOB SEARCH FOCUS OR AT LEAST YOUR BEST GUESS

Today, I promise to go to a bookstore to see how topics are organized. I promise to go to the library and learn how organizations are classified.

List below your best guess of what occupations you want to do in the future (up to three):

_____

_____

_____

List your best guess of what Standard of Industry Codes (SIC) or North American Industry Classification System (NAICS) you want to target (up to ten). You will eventually be matching up names of organizations as potential employers that are classified by your interests. If you need help with this, ask your local reference librarian for guidance. They are great!

SIC	NAICS

Occupational Ideas

MY BEST GUESS

1	2	3

Primary Category				
Sub-Category	SIC Interest	SIC Interest	SIC Interest	SIC Interest

Know What You Want?
Organizations I Admire

IDEA #19

THE BASICS: CREATE A TARGET ORGANIZATION LIST

IDEA #19 THE BASICS: CREATE A TARGET ORGANIZATION LIST

Initially, your target organization list might be more important than your updated resume because this list helps others help you get introductions into potential employers BEFORE there is a job opening. By getting in before there is a job opening, there is no competition!

Your target organization list will start out like a resume. Your contact information will be at the top followed by a brief summary of who you are and what you are targeting occupationally. Your list of two to three columns of prospective employers follows. Include up to 100 employers. Keep in mind that more is not necessarily better because you will be asking others what they know about these organizations and who they know.

There are several ways to build your target organization list. If you are targeting non-profits, start by going to the United Way's website. It lists the organizations to which they contribute. There are non-profit associations that can help you build your list, as well as directories at your local library.

For a quick search about any organization, go to your preferred search engine and type in phrases like this: "machine shop companies in Indianapolis" or "organizations for children in St. Louis." and the results of your searches will build your short list quickly.

Find out what business organization databases are available at your local library. My favorite database is Million Dollar Database by Dun and Bradstreet (D & B), although there are many more good ones. What I like about the Million Dollar Database is you can sort by many features including SIC or NAICS, keyword, zip code, and dollar amount in revenues. You can even sort by keywords. You can export information from this database into an excel spreadsheet for easy reference.

Do note that as soon as any database is published, it's out of date. Be sure to call to verify the decision maker's name before making initial contact. Nothing is more embarrassing than asking to speak to a person who died three years ago, yet is still listed in the database you are using!

INTENTION
Guide my actions today as I give myself permission to explore. Let me remember that this is just a starting point, subject to change. Help me to think of this as a field trip where I can learn and decide what organizations are right for me. Amen!

ACTION
Today I promise to select organizations that I will put on my target list.

IDEA #19 THE BASICS: CREATE A TARGET ORGANIZATION LIST

Today I promise to select organizations that I will put on my target list.

Make a list of your top 30 to 100 organizations by reading newspapers, business journals, doing an online search of the "Top 100 Companies in _____(city)." Experiment with different ways to compile your list. Experiment with learning more about organizations in your area by using SIC or NAICS. Do not worry if these organizations have job openings or not. This is a strategy for developing a pro-active search before there are job openings.

_____   _____

_____   _____

_____   _____

_____   _____

_____   _____

_____   _____

_____   _____

_____   _____

_____   _____

_____   _____

_____   _____

_____   _____

_____   _____

_____   _____

IDEA #20

KEEP YOUR PROMISES – OPTIMISM BUILDERS

IDEA #20 KEEP YOUR PROMISES — OPTIMISM BUILDERS

Feeling good about yourself can be as simple as keeping your promises and then noticing. That's why including a job search success team in a career transition plan is so important. You are creating tangible evidence that you are not sitting still, and you are recording it in your career transition journal.

A job search is the ultimate in delayed gratification. Focus on action taken and promises kept, not the results of your action. So many things are out of your control. Will they return your calls? Will they like you? Will they bring you back for a second interview? If you focus on what you cannot control, the optimism that you've built will fade. If you want to build optimism, keep your promises. If you haven't completed the ACTION steps in IDEAS #1 through 14, it's time to go back and begin, even if it's the same Action step you take for several days in a row.

Keep a journal and write in it daily. Write down the promises you have kept, promises you are fixing to get ready to do, promises you can do alone, and promises you will do with the support of others. Journals are very handy because you can whine, complain, or rage to your heart's content. (That way those negative feelings are less likely to be expressed during a job interview.) Write about your successes, too. This journal is for you. Something happens when you write honestly about how your day is going. It often gives you insight on what to do next. In my experience, job hunters find work faster and with less suffering if they commit to journaling daily.

INTENTION

Help me to keep my promises today. Let me focus more on what I can control and less on what I can't. Thank you for the opportunity to write down my feelings, successes, mistakes, and my dreams. Amen!

ACTION

Today I promise to buy a journal and write in it daily.

IDEA #20 KEEP YOUR PROMISES – OPTIMISM BUILDERS

Today I promise to buy a journal and write in it daily.

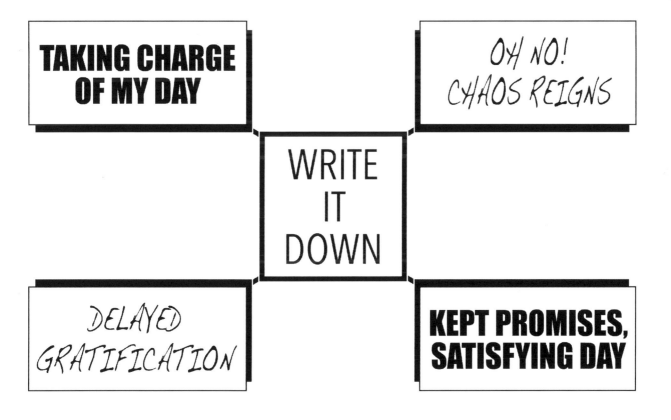

IDEA #21

IF YOU USE IT, DON'T LOSE IT

IDEA #21 IF YOU USE IT, DON'T LOSE IT

You are right at the edge of moving away from preparation to actually talking to people. Before you switch gears, get organized. If you don't have a way to track what action you are going to take, it will be difficult to retrieve information later when you need it.

Some people make piles. Great! You might want to organize your piles by the three markets you are targeting. Some people make folders of the people they have contacted with the date, person's name, title, and organization on the tab. Some people buy a two-inch binder and put an alphabetical index inside. Some people use contact databases like Outlook. There is no right or wrong way and it doesn't matter how you organize yourself. What matters is you can easily access information when you need it.

Take a look back to IDEA #8 about setting up your job search headquarters. Where are you going to put your stuff? Remember to stay out of the basement for long periods of time. If that's where your headquarters are, then buy a portable file case that you can bring upstairs. If possible, work at the table where there is a window.

Some job searchers over-organize to avoid actually talking to people. Some job searchers under-organize because anything to do with paper just sucks the life out of them. Check your motives as you put together an information retrieval system. Either way, it might help to limit your time in this activity to no more than 15 to 20 minutes a day. That's more than enough time to organize each day without hindering other essential job search activities. For you under-organizers, limit your time to 10 to 15 minutes a day until you've built up a tolerance for using an information retrieval system.

INTENTION
Help me to put together an information retrieval system that is easy for me to use. Give me strength to be willing to put things away so I can find them later. Give me strength to be willing to actually talk to people I may not know. Amen!

ACTION
My promise today is to breathe and relax as I build my workable information retrieval system.

IDEA #21 IF YOU USE IT, DON'T LOSE IT

My promise today is to breathe and relax as I build my workable information retrieval system.

Where are you going to put your stuff? Make it easy and simple to retrieve it later.

IDEA #22

FIND THE GOOD AND WRITE IT DOWN

IDEA #22 FIND THE GOOD AND WRITE IT DOWN

There may be an ongoing dialogue in your head about how inadequate you are. It is a nasty, non-productive conversation where nobody wins. Even some of the most successful people have an ongoing dialogue about how inadequate they are. Truth is, each of us is good at some things, bad at others, and some areas are not yet developed. The negative inner conversation may never go away; take care of yourself anyway. Are you eating nutritiously, sleeping enough, and going outside? Review your list of 20 self-care activities (see IDEAS #3 and 4). It's important to have your self-care plan in place because the negative inner conversation may get louder as you make the decision to move into the Action phase of your job search. That's okay, just continue your self-care plan and keep going.

Job Seekers who are discouraged may erroneously conclude that they do not have any accomplishments. Remember, depression is a liar. If that's how you are feeling, it's time to go look for high energy moments from your life. Start by looking at your past and finding things that went well.

What was working then?
What skills did you enjoy?

Find times in your life that you enjoyed what you were doing, did it well, and felt pride doing it. These serve as proof that you really can do what you say you can. Once you've written them down, give copies to your job search support team (see IDEA #11). That way, they can remind you of what you enjoy when you forget. It will be a comfort to you.

These proofs are also what you want to use during job interviewing. Often during a job interview, you will get this question: "Can you give me an example of something you accomplished?"

These proofs (memories of positive experiences) will be helpful when you conduct career research meetings to determine where you fit in today's market. Some of these positive experiences might end up on your resume. If you genuinely don't have any proofs, then fall back to your capabilities and aptitudes, which could be natural abilities that have not been developed yet. For instance, you may have an aptitude for filmmaking but have never done it. Talking about aptitudes are indicators of your future success and you may find an employer who is willing to train you. Career research meetings will help you discover which employers those are.

INTENTION
Guide my memory to help me to write down 5 or more stories that can serve as proof of my abilities. Give me the courage to look inside by completing this phrase: "I remember a time when I...." Give me a quiet heart to remember times that I enjoyed. Let me be open to surrounding myself with a support team to remind me of who I am. Amen!

ACTION
My promise today is to look inside and find specific examples of my natural abilities.

IDEA #22 FIND THE GOOD AND WRITE IT DOWN

My promise today is to look inside and find specific examples of my natural abilities.

Write down 5 true stories about yourself where you enjoyed what you were doing. You may notice an un-spoken rule that says, "Hey, it's not okay to brag about yourself." Brag anyway. Gently allow memories of work-related activities to come up where you took action and write them down. If you can't remember any work-related activities, then write about actions you took in your leisure time.

Begin by saying, "I remember a time when…."

_____

_____

_____

_____

_____

_____

_____

_____

_____

_____

_____

_____

_____

_____

_____

IDEA #23

THE BASICS:
USING CAREER RESEARCH MEETINGS
TO OVERCOME OBSTACLES
(REAL OR PERCEIVED)

IDEA #23 THE BASICS:
USING CAREER RESEARCH MEETINGS TO OVERCOME OBSTACLES
(REAL OR PERCEIVED)

You may be painfully aware of issues that have held you back from finding work. These may include:

1. A lack of occupational focus.
2. Burn out from being in a "wrong fit" job.
3. You just moved here and you don't know anyone. You're isolated.
4. You took yourself off the market for more than six months because of illness, depression, or family issue.
5. Your self-confidence is shot.
6. You have a new occupational focus but you don't know anyone who does it.
7. You think you are too old, too young, too fat, too male, too female, too black, or too white.
8. You don't have access to the "good old boy" network.
9. You went to the wrong high school or the wrong college. You have the wrong degree. You don't have a college degree.
10. There are not enough jobs because of the lousy economy.
11. It is too scary to leave the same life-sucking occupation you have always been in.
12. Your spouse would not approve of you re-inventing yourself.
13. Your mother always wanted you to be an attorney and you don't want to let her down.
14. You will lose your house if you don't find work in 90 days.

These are called "stoppers," and without a plan you might throw up your hands and say, "What's the use?" That could be the end of the story, but it doesn't have to be. The purpose of career research meetings is to identify real or perceived obstacles, and develop ways to move forward anyway.

Career research meetings are not about asking others for a job. Career research meetings are not about telling everyone you know that you are looking for work. It's about testing your career ideas against actual market conditions and enlisting potential employers into your cause.

Think of yourself as a solution for some employer's challenge. But right now you are a solution that is untried, unproven, and unknown. Career research meetings are like market research where you gather market-specific information to determine how to overcome obstacles. Career research meetings will help you identify strategies that are valid, reasonable, and achievable!

INTENTION

Let me believe that I can turn around my current job search. Guide my actions, as I give myself permission to approach the job market in a different way. Amen!

ACTION

My promise is to see myself with assets and deficits, a beautiful weaving of being uniquely human. My promise is to be willing to be of service to a future employer.

IDEA #23 THE BASICS:
USING CAREER RESEARCH MEETINGS TO OVERCOME OBSTACLES (REAL OR PERCEIVED)

My promise is to see myself with assets and deficits, a beautiful weaving of being uniquely human. My promise is to be willing to be of service to a future employer.

STOPPERS

Write down 5 things that hold you back.

_____
_____
_____
_____
_____

THINK

Write 5 strategies / "go-arounds" to keep the stoppers from stopping you.

_____
_____
_____
_____
_____

GO

Write down 7 talents or skills you want to use in the future.

_____
_____
_____
_____
_____
_____
_____

IDEA #24

THE BASICS: USING CAREER RESEARCH MEETINGS TO REINVENT YOURSELF

IDEA #24 THE BASICS: USING CAREER RESEARCH MEETINGS TO REINVENT YOURSELF

If you have been knocking your head against the wall by ONLY applying for jobs and not getting any responses, then it is time to stop knocking your head against the wall. You have no control over whether or not someone will bring you in for a job interview. You do have control over conducting career research meetings to reinvent yourself.

You may assume it's your age, but after conducting career research meetings you may find it wasn't your age; instead, the problem might have been the way you dress and talk. Those can be fixed! If you have validated that age is a factor, compensatory strategies can be put in place. The beauty of career research meetings is you get to check out your assumptions. In order for career research meetings to be valid, you need to talk to 4 to 6 qualified people at different organizations to determine if you are getting the same information. If you only receive feedback from ONE person, that is just one person's opinion. However, if you get the same information from several different sources, then chances are the research is sound. Your career research meetings may give you information that you have significant barriers to overcome. Or your career research meetings may tell you that the hurdles are mostly self-imposed.

Regardless of the results, YOU get to choose what to do with this information. One of my clients received feedback from 20 different people that the career trajectory he wanted to achieve was not possible; yet, he kept conducting career research meetings until he found a way to get around the obstacle. Yes, it took him longer, but he ended up doing exactly what he wanted to do.

The bigger the career change, the longer it may take. For instance, if you are an accountant and you want to become a veterinarian, it will take a few of years to retool. If that is the case, finding interim work while you go to school may be your focus.

The point of career research meetings is to NOT GUESS. You can avoid costly mistakes. For instance, one person I know pursued a Master of Business degree only to discover that the industry he was targeting did not value this advanced degree. He spent all that money and ended up taking his MBA information off his resume just to get hired.

Ideally, it helps to have an occupational focus to test. However, some job hunters start their career research meetings with a single question such as: "What kind of occupations would you recommend if I want to work alone?" My challenge to you is what would your question be? What do you want to learn?

INTENTION
Let me be willing to try career research meetings. Guide my actions, as I give myself permission to approach the job market in a different way. Amen!

ACTION
My promise is to think through what I want my career research project to be.

IDEA #24 THE BASICS: USING CAREER RESEARCH MEETINGS TO REINVENT YOURSELF

My promise is to think through what I want my career research project to be.

Imagine that you are the one walking through the door of opportunity.

IDEA #25

JUMP IN – THE WATER IS FINE!

IDEA #25 JUMP IN – THE WATER IS FINE!

You don't have to know exactly what you want to do next, but it does help to have some ideas. Developing your ideas on a document will give others a glimpse of your positive future. A Career Research Ideas document starts out looking very similar to a resume. You have your name, phone number, and email address at the top. A summary only of your background that is pertinent to your future is underneath. Then your document shifts to telling the reader what occupations you are exploring and what organizations you want to learn about. Your Career Research Ideas document then lists 30 to 100 potential employers. Your Career Research Ideas document is also called a Target Company list.

How do you use this list? First, you show this document to people you may already know to get introductions. Secondly, you will show it to people you don't know. Cold calling is when you contact someone without the benefit of an introduction, and warm calling is when you contact someone with the benefit of an introduction. How brave are you feeling?

For some of you, contacting people you DON'T KNOW feels less risky. These might include pastors, rabbis, Rotary club presidents, city leaders, newspaper reporters, and chamber of commerce directors. You can have a compelling conversation about your future without them having any preconceived notion about what you did in the past.

For some of you, contacting people you DO KNOW feels less risky. These might include your hair stylist or barber, next-door neighbor, best friend from high school, college roommate, former co-workers, alumni association, people you know from clubs, relatives; and people you know from your church, synagogue, or mosque. If you give your Career Research Ideas document to your relatives, be sure to train them what to say and what not to say when they pass it on.

I had a client who found work because his wife told her hair stylist what kind of work her husband was seeking, and it just so happened that the hairstylist's previous customer was hiring for the very same occupation! You can create this kind of luck, too.

Where will you begin? With people you know, or with people you don't know?

INTENTION
Give me the courage to become known to others. Amen!

ACTION
Today I promise to make a list of people I want to contact first, second, and third. I will share my Career Research Ideas document with people who are likely to introduce me to others.

IDEA #25 JUMP IN – THE WATER IS FINE!

Today I promise to make a list of people I want to contact first, second, and third. I will share my Career Research Ideas document with people who are likely to introduce me to others.

What one scary job search activity will you do today? Pretend you are in a Halloween haunted house...you are supposed to be scared but take action anyway.

IDEA #26

THE BASICS: LET OTHERS KNOW WHO YOU ARE, AND HOW THEY CAN HELP

IDEA #26 THE BASICS: LET OTHERS KNOW WHO YOU ARE, AND HOW THEY CAN HELP

(Note: This is sometimes called level one script and is designed to generate introductions into your target companies.)

After you've developed a summary of who you are and what you want to attract, make a list of 10 people you personally know who can help you fine-tune your presentation. Choose safe people who can give you positive feedback as you get more proficient in telling your story. These might include your barber, hair stylist, next-door neighbor, friend you know from the coffee shop, best friend from college, and former co-workers. Don't include family members at first. If you have been isolating yourself, then hang out at a coffee shop, go to a job search support group, or join a Rotary or Toastmasters Club until you become a familiar face. Even in practice sessions, keep track of real introductions you obtain. Very soon, you will be actually contacting the introductions you have received and expanding your circle of who knows you.

It is time to enlist others into your cause. You might start with something like this:

1. For the past ___ years, I have been working as_____.
2. (Insert a brief summary of only the part of your past you wish to repeat) I particularly enjoyed _____. (Example: coming up with new solutions that were more time efficient and user friendly.)
3. I am at a point in my career where I would like to take on new challenges. I'm looking for introductions into these organizations to determine if they would be a good fit for me.

   a. Please take a look at my Target Company list and tell me what you know about each of them, particularly what you know about each company's reputation.
   b. Review the list again and tell me what companies you think are missing.
   c. Who do you know that works there? (Show your list again.)
   d. How do you know this person, and may I use your name when I reach out to them?
   e. May I keep you informed and give you an update in a few weeks?
4. Here's a hard copy. I'll send you my target list electronically if you want to pass it on. Please keep me in mind when you hear of anything.
5. This has been very helpful. Is there anything I can do for you?

Now memorize what you want to say about yourself, and what questions you want to ask. You may feel resistance, but ask anyway. By first contacting people who are not employers, it's safer for you to make mistakes until you get better at this. You may get genuine introductions. Be open to that!

INTENTION
Give me the courage to come out of hiding. Give me the strength to practice saying aloud what I want to do and what organizations I'd like to learn more about. Amen!

ACTION
My promise today is to let one person know who I am, and what I am exploring, and ask for referrals. Then I will do it again. I will practice with people who are not threatening to me.

IDEA #26 THE BASICS: LET OTHERS KNOW WHO YOU ARE, AND HOW THEY CAN HELP

My promise today is to let one person know who I am, and what I am exploring, and ask for referrals. Then I will do it again. I will practice with people who are not threatening to me.

Describe how your Target Company list will make it easier for you to get introductions:

_____

_____

_____

_____

_____

_____

_____

_____

_____

_____

_____

_____

_____

_____

IDEA #27

THE BASICS: WHAT? DON'T TELL PEOPLE I'M LOOKING FOR A JOB?

IDEA #27 THE BASICS: WHAT? DON'T TELL PEOPLE I'M LOOKING FOR A JOB?

(Note: This is an alternative level one script based your occupational focus. It can also be combined with IDEA #26's script)

You want to build support and alliances in your career transition journey. What you say to others (and to yourself) will make a huge difference. Keep it simple. A brief summary of your background, followed by what you enjoy doing, is enough. Don't talk about failures, disappointments, or bitterness. If you are targeting something you are inexperienced in, DON'T start your sentence with: "While I have no experience in this field, I know I could do a good job." That's presumptuous and starts the conversation off on the wrong foot. Instead try the script below.

Just fill in the sentences below and you are well on your way to having a great way to introduce yourself:

1. For the past __ years, I've been doing_____.
2. What I've enjoyed about my work is (list three things you are good at).
3. Give a transitional statement. Something like this: I'm ready for my next step and I'm exploring options.
4. Then give occupational ideas or goals.
   a. I would like to get more experience in: (or)
   b. I would like to learn more about how... (or)
   c. I would like to continue my work as...

5. Because I am in the research phase of my search I am not looking for a job at this point. Instead, I am seeking concrete information on where my best point of entry could be.
6. Who do you know that does similar work? (or) Who would you suggest I talk with to learn more about _____?
7. How do you know them?
8. May I use your name when I contact them?
9. Thank you! I'll touch base with you in a few weeks and let you know what happened.

Practice this script until it becomes second nature to you. Then you can use it whenever you interact with people.

INTENTION
Thank you for giving me the tools to reach out to more people. Help me to understand I do not have to do it perfectly. Guide my actions so that I stop being the best kept secret around! Amen.

ACTION
My promise is to find 10 people, even if they are strangers, and practice my script. I will have paper and pen with me, so when I get real introductions I will be able to write them down.

IDEA #27 THE BASICS: WHAT? DON'T TELL PEOPLE I'M LOOKING FOR A JOB?

My promise is to find 10 people, even if they are strangers, and practice my script.

I will have paper and pen with me, so when I get real introductions I will be able to write them down.

Write down how frequently you will be practicing your script.

Also, write down your feelings about reaching out to others. Scared? Excited?

_____

_____

_____

_____

_____

_____

_____

_____

_____

_____

IDEA #28

**IF YOU DON'T ASK,
THE ANSWER IS ALWAYS "NO".
ASK. THE ANSWER MIGHT BE "YES!"**

IDEA #28 IF YOU DON'T ASK, THE ANSWER IS ALWAYS "NO". ASK. THE ANSWER MIGHT BE "YES!"

Can news articles be leveraged to get you a face-to-face meeting? Yes. Think about what you want to accomplish. If you found a news article about one of your target companies, how would you use it to meet someone new? What did you learn in the article that made you want to learn more? Let's say the article mentions a key contact name of someone who could potentially lead you to your next step. Think beyond the immediate information in the article. What are you personally curious about? What do you have in common with the person who wrote the article? What do you want to learn? What's in it for the contact person to see you?

There are three ways to approach this person:

1. Write a fan letter.
2. Write what you have in common and request a meeting to learn more (informational meeting).
3. Send the person mentioned a different article that further strengthens the points made in the original article and send it is as a "thought you would enjoy" gift.

Now comes the scary part: writing and actually sending a letter (or email) to a stranger. Once you do this, wait three to five days before you call the person and ask for a face-to-face meeting. First reference the letter you sent. Ask to see them anyway even if they don't remember receiving your letter.

Why would a total stranger be willing to see you? What do you bring to these discussions that may appeal to this stranger? Think this through. Remember, a stranger is often happy to share their insights, if you are sincere in your approach.

At the same time, be prepared to reassure the contact person that you only want to learn; you're not hitting them up for a job. This assurance will often overcome the person's resistance to seeing you when they are not familiar with the informational meeting approach.

Be clear about what you want to learn before you make your approach. Remember, if you don't write, you won't learn. If you don't ask for a meeting, you are self-selecting yourself out. If you don't ask, the answer is always, "No."

INTENTION
Give me the courage to risk writing to a total stranger. If I feel unworthy, let me ask anyway. Let me ask, even if the person I ask might say "No." Amen!

ACTION
My promise is to find an article in a Business Journal or newspaper that is about one of my target markets. Just for fun, I will write a letter to the author of the article or a contact person mentioned in the article. Then I promise to follow-up by phone and ask to meet.

IDEA #28 IF YOU DON'T ASK, THE ANSWER IS ALWAYS "NO." ASK. THE ANSWER MIGHT BE "YES!"

My promise is to find an article in a Business Journal or newspaper that is about one of my target markets. Just for fun, I will write a letter to the author of the article or to a contact person mentioned in the article. Then I promise to follow-up by phone and ask to meet.

Remember as a child when you went on field trips? Write about how reaching out to a person from an article is like going on a field trip.

_____

_____

_____

_____

_____

_____

_____

_____

_____

_____

_____

_____

_____

_____

_____

_____

IDEA #29

ADVICE AND INFORMATION
MEETINGS ARE NOT BUSY WORK

IDEA #29 ADVICE AND INFORMATION MEETINGS ARE NOT BUSY WORK

Advice and information meetings are similar to career research meetings. Some use these terms interchangeably. For me, the purpose of career research meetings is to validate that you are on the right track. Then you want to go deeper. You want a job, right? You want quality job interviews, right? Why bother adding an extra step by talking to business leaders BEFORE there is a job opening? The short answer is that by adding this step, your job search actually goes faster and will be more productive.

By conducting advice and information meetings, you go deeper to:

1. Get insider information that you later use to possibly create a position
2. Get insider information that you can use later during a job interview
3. Enlist powerful people into your cause
4. Get referrals to other professionals or associations

Initially, when you start meeting with people it may feel like you are just out there meeting your community, that it isn't leading anywhere, and it isn't getting you any closer to a job. Keep going, anyway. There is a principle of momentum at work here, and if you quit before hitting critical mass, you will miss out on opportunities that can only be discovered through advice and information meetings. It is not busy work.

Yes, it may be scary or awkward at first. No, you won't embarrass yourself if you prepare in advance. Yes, you may get rejected, but not as often as applying for jobs and never hearing back. In an advice and information meeting, you have an 85% to 95% chance of being seen if you have a trustworthy person to introduce you. This is a much more efficient use of your time.

Be open to the chance that the relationships you build will give a potential employer an "audition" without the pressure of a job opening. Think about it from the employer's point of view. A 30- minute advice and information meeting will give the employer access to potential talent without paying a recruiter or sorting through hundreds of applicants. If the referral source is strong enough, you have an implied endorsement.

Think about advice and information meeting as if you were dating. You wouldn't go up to a perfect stranger and say, "Will you marry me?" Instead, advice and information meetings, like dating, move a relationship forward in a meaningful way, so that you get to know each other and find out if there is anything worth pursuing.

INTENTION
Let me be willing to add advice and information meetings to my job search plan. Guide my actions as I approach my job search in a different way. Amen!

ACTION
My promise is to expand my knowledge about my target markets even when I am in the practice stage of advice and information meetings.

IDEA #29 ADVICE AND INFORMATION MEETINGS ARE NOT BUSY WORK

My promise is to expand my knowledge about my target markets even when I am in the practice stage of advice and information meetings.

Write down any resistance you might be feeling about reaching out to actual people who work at one of your target organizations. Does it make sense to add this job search tool to your overall job search strategy? If it does make sense, how will you get better at information meetings?

Hint: Practice!

_____

_____

_____

_____

_____

_____

_____

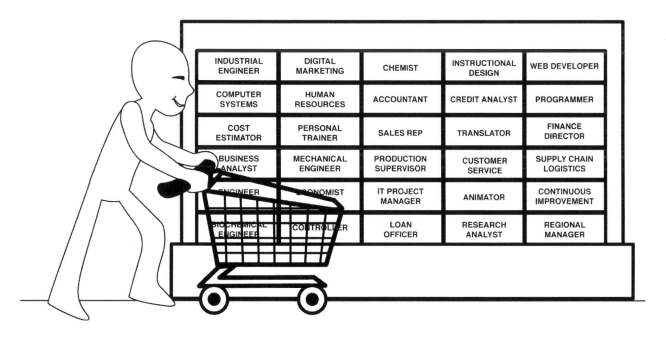

IDEA #30

THE BASICS: FOR AN ADVICE AND INFORMATION MEETING

IDEA #30 THE BASICS: FOR AN ADVICE AND INFORMATION MEETING

(Note: A level two script is designed to validate your ideas and get further introductions.)

Here are some basic questions to facilitate an advice and information meeting:

1. What do you enjoy about your work?
2. How long have you been with XYZ organization?
3. Where do you fit into the overall organizational structure?
4. What is the company's culture like?

5. Here's where I see myself fitting [state your occupational focus idea], where do you see me fitting?
6. Am I qualified? If not, why not? How do I overcome this obstacle?
7. What is the salary range for this position?
8. If you were in my shoes, what would you advise me to do next?

9. Who within your company would be a good person to talk to learn more?
10. Who would you recommend outside of your organization?
11. May I use your name as a source of introduction? How do you know her / him?

12. Thank you. This has been very useful. What may I do for you? And may I keep you informed of my progress? Great! I will touch base with you in a few weeks to bring you up to date.

When you receive answers to your questions, you can make an informed decision about if this employer is right for you. If not, YOU get to reject them! The face-to-face meetings will focus your efforts by discerning what companies you wish to keep. Firsthand information is always better than reading about a company in a book.

It's not that different from buying a car. First, you decide what you need in a car, and then you research and ask good questions from experts in the field. Then you take the car on a test drive. You invest in the car that works best for your needs. The same process works when shopping for the right employer. You get to be in the driver's seat.

INTENTION
Help me to imagine that I can be in the driver's seat. Give me the wisdom to become better known through advice and information meetings. Amen!

ACTION
My promise is to write my top 7 to 12 questions I will ask in an advice and information meeting.

IDEA #30 THE BASICS: QUESTIONS FOR AN ADVICE AND INFORMATION MEETING

My promise is to write my top 7 to 12 questions I will to ask in an advice and information meeting.

Fill in the blank rectangles with "must have" descriptors important to you regarding your future employer.

_____

_____

_____

_____

_____

_____

_____

_____

_____

_____

_____

IDEA #31

NETWORKING PRINCIPLES WHEN YOU FEEL LIKE HIDING

IDEA #31 NETWORKING PRINCIPLES WHEN YOU FEEL LIKE HIDING

Have you noticed that you aren't extroverted when you are despondent? Yet, in order for you to job search effectively, doing extroverted activities like networking (an informational interaction) is important. You may end up having to bribe yourself (chocolate can be nice or a warm bath afterward), but figure out a way to interact with people.

Depending on which study you look at, 63% to 82% of all opportunities are found through networking. Yikes! You don't have to LIKE networking, but I would recommend you include it in the mix. By reaching out and meeting with other people, you have an opportunity to focus on them instead of any negativity.

Networking often brings out the best in people. Networking is reciprocal. Networking is NOT bothering people, particularly if your sacred intention is to be of service, in addition to receiving information and referrals from them. Occasionally, you will meet a jerk. That's okay. Just let it go and move on. Why network? To:

1. Learn more about market-specific information and your target industries to make you a more astute job interviewer later.
2. Learn what barriers may present themselves in making a career change and how to overcome them.
3. Position yourself to create a position by addressing an employer's unmet needs.
4. Unearth unadvertised job leads.
5. Get to know the market better as the market gets to know you.
6. Find firsthand information like salary ranges so when the offer comes, you are better prepared to negotiate.
7. Be of service to others as they are of service to you.
8. Leverage information and increase your perceived value.
9. Develop lifelong strategic business relationships.
10. Talk to people 3 to 10 years ahead of you to get clearer about your career path.

Recommended readings: *The Introvert's Advantage* by Marty Laney and *Savvy Networking* by Susan RoAne. Hint: if you read both these books, you can delay networking for another week!

INTENTION
Help me to overcome any reluctance to networking. Guide my actions so that I may be of service to others, even when I'm down. Be with me, when I send that letter, when I follow-up, when I set the appointment, and when I actually leave the house and meet someone. Protect me from feelings of defeat if the meeting didn't go as planned. Amen!

ACTION
My promise is to become better known and tell others about what I am targeting. If any day gets too overwhelming, my promise is to go to a coffee shop and talk to one person anyway.

IDEA #31 NETWORKING PRINCIPLES WHEN YOU FEEL LIKE HIDING

My promise is to become better known and tell others about what I am targeting. If any day gets too overwhelming, my promise is to go to a coffee shop and talk to one person anyway.

If you are extremely shy, practice by going into a small retail shop and act as if you are a customer. You will get better at information meetings (networking) by asking two questions:

1. What do you enjoy about your work?
2. How long have you worked here?

Next say, "That's nice" or "That's too bad" (if they don't enjoy their work) depending on their answer. Then say, "I just started a job search and I want to learn more about [occupation]. Do you know anyone who does that?"

If they actually know someone say: "Well, if you don't mind I'd like to introduce myself to that person so I can learn more. May I get your contact information as a way to introduce myself? And by the way, how do you know this person?" Write down the information, hand them your business card and thank them.

If they don't know anyone, hand them your business card and ask permission for them to keep you in mind when they hear of any information they believe might help you.

Congratulations! You've just practiced an information meeting. Now go to a different shop and repeat this process two more times (or as many times as needed to feel comfortable with this 4 question information meeting). Reward yourself despite how lousy or awkward you were. What's important is you modeled success behavior for finding work. Keep practicing until you get the hang of it. Don't feel obligated to buy anything. And only choose times that are not busy.

IDEA #32

THE BASICS: HOW TO WORK A ROOM AT A NETWORKING EVENT

IDEA #32 THE BASICS: HOW TO WORK A ROOM AT A NETWORKING EVENT

At a networking event, you are seeking information. Your goal is to talk to at least 3 people.

WRONG "Hi, I'm Sarah, and I'm looking for work in operations management. Who do you know that needs a good operations manager?" DON'T ASK WHERE THE JOB OPENINGS ARE.
Instead, you want to probe for mutual interests:

RIGHT "Hi, I'm Sarah, and I'm curious, how is effectiveness measured within your organization?" Then depending on the response you might say, "Are you satisfied with the level of productivity your operations is producing?" If the person you are talking to isn't the decision maker, then you can ask who is. ALWAYS ASK FOR INFORMATION, and do not ask for a job.

Within the time span of less than three minutes, you've completed a mini-advice and information meeting. If the person you are talking to is a good fit for your mutual interests, you can then say, "Wow, it sounds like we have a lot in common. Would you mind if we set up a time to get together over breakfast to continue this conversation?"

Then you exchange business cards, set a meeting time, and then move to the next person that is appealing. Using this process, you will talk to several people in a single event. Talk about efficient! If no one is appealing to you, then hang around the coffee station and welcome a person as he / she fills up his / her coffee. Do not get bogged down with any one person. Here is another script:

1. Hi, I am Chris Rodriquez, and you are?
2. What brings you to this event?
www.CourageousChange.net

3. Tell me about what you do.
4. What do you enjoy about your work?

This four-step process will let you quickly ascertain if the person you are interacting with can benefit your search. If not, quickly excuse yourself and move on. You could say, "If you don't mind, there are a couple of other people I want to get to before the program starts. It was nice meeting you."

Trust me, you will find work faster if you don't ask for a job directly. Remember knowledge is power and the more you know firsthand from experts who know, the more likely you can use this information to your benefit. Your goal in working a room is to set the follow-up appointment to learn more later, not monopolize someone's time at the event. From start to finish, your interactions will take 5 to 7 minutes per person; I promise that you won't feel hurried. Be present. Be courageous. Don't forget to hide in the bathroom if you'd like before approaching the next person! Just don't stay there.

A good read to strengthen your networking abilities is Jeffrey Gitomer's *Little Black Book of Connections: 6.5 Assets for Networking Your Way to RICH Relationships*

INTENTION
Thank you for giving me hope that I can interact with more people. Guide my actions today and give me a willingness to change. Amen!

ACTION
My promise today is to practice how to work a room.

IDEA #32 THE BASICS: HOW TO WORK A ROOM AT A NETWORKING EVENT

My promise today is to practice how to work a room.

Draw a treasure map or a maze. Insert where the safe zones are (bathroom or by the coffee table). Insert where the prize will be (where you get the most information). Insert where the neutral zones will be (asking the host if you may help or put your back to an existing conversation and listen in). Remember to breathe! Your quest is to talk with 3 people with the goal of setting up one follow-up appointment.

IDEA #33

WHEN BUILDING A PERFECT RESUME WILL SLOW YOU DOWN

IDEA #33 WHEN BUILDING A PERFECT RESUME WILL SLOW YOU DOWN

Why do so many people get scared when it comes to writing the perfect resume? Why do you think that getting the resume absolutely right will help you? So much pressure! For a resume to accurately represent you, it needs to be in your words. The good resume writers use your words. The bad resume writers put words in your resume that you would never say. Secondly, your resume needs to be free of spelling errors and grammatical errors. Ask 3 people (who are attentive to detail and accuracy) to review your resume before you send it out.

A resume is important, but remember it is a tactical tool, not an overall strategy. If you think that the resume and only the resume will help you get hired, think again. What will get you hired is getting in front of the right person, at the right time, with the right set of engaging communication skills.

When you conduct career research meetings, you don't necessarily have to have a resume, but I do recommend that you have a few occupational ideas. This requires brainstorming and narrowing those ideas to a working hypothesis. What is your best guess of where you see yourself fitting into today's market? If you are one of those people who could do anything, your brain will eventually explode with all those possibilities and scatter all over the landscape like confetti after a parade. Less is better. Take the time to create no more than 3 occupational targets.

Don't constantly tweak your resume. It can take hours and hours to individualize a resume for too many targets, hours that could be used more productively somewhere else. On the other hand, if the best you can do for now is to build a resume that is based on your dominant skills and aptitudes, that's okay. A resume is about your future, not your past. A resume that dumps your entire work history will not get you where you want to be. A resume does not have to represent more than 15 years of experience. You get to choose.

If there are parts of your past that you never want to repeat again, don't put it in your resume. If you have skills and knowledge that you despise, don't put it in your resume. A resume doesn't always need to be chronological. Use cover letters to adapt information. Sometimes it's better to use a cover letter with career highlights than to use a resume, particularly if you are changing careers. You get to control the information going out. You get to talk about experiences you enjoyed.

INTENTION
Help me to not get bogged down in creating the perfect resume. Guide my efforts to create an excellent resume. Help me find 3 people to check for spelling and grammatical errors before I send it out. Amen!

ACTION
I promise to go to the library and check out two books on how to write a resume.

IDEA #33 WHEN BUILDING A PERFECT RESUME WILL SLOW YOU DOWN

I promise to go to the library and check out two books on how to write a resume.

If you choose to hire someone to write your resume for you, be careful that it is written like the way you speak. Yes, it's okay to insert industry words to make your resume more searchable, but not at the expense of sounding like a thousand other resumes. Who will help you edit your resume? Remember your resume will start with a focus or summary of what you are seeking and everything that follows must support that focus.

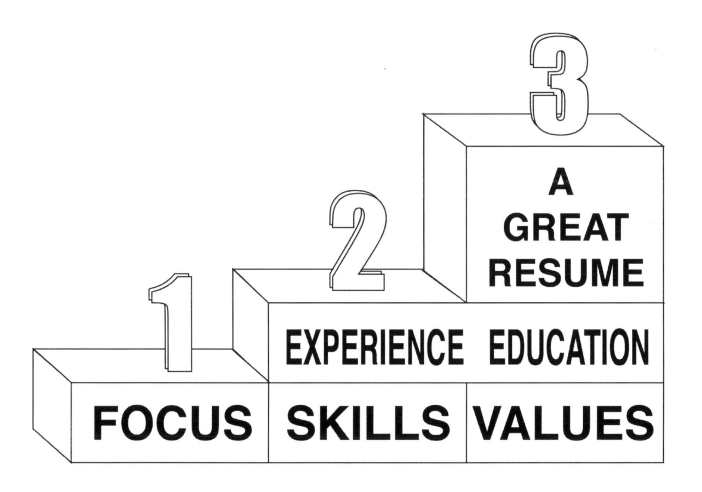

IDEA #34

CHANGE YOUR IMAGE:
SAY NICE THINGS. LOOK NICE, TOO.

IDEA #34 CHANGE YOUR IMAGE: SAY NICE THINGS. LOOK NICE, TOO.

If you have been using social media like Facebook to let the world know how disgruntled and depressed you are, STOP NOW. Social media is for strengthening your credentials, not to have people feel sorry for you.

You want people to want to help and introduce you to people on your Career Research list. If you have created an online image of being a dejected complainer, it may take several weeks of corrective, positive posts before you can reach out to your online community for additional information. Some employers actually require access to your Facebook account before you are hired. Make it a rule to think of social media as a public forum, not a private one.

Then there is the issue of chronic complaining. If you are using words that demand the listener to respond by saying, "Oh, that's terrible" you are playing the "ain't-it-awful" game. Stay away from "ain't-it-awful" people, and please don't try to drag someone down by playing that game, too. You may have been victimized, but to tell that story repeatedly will only attract an employer who will victimize you again. Whenever you feel like telling your sad story to someone who could potentially help you, mention three things that you are grateful for instead.

Now look in the mirror and put your hands over your head. Then smile, even if you don't mean it. Part of becoming an attractive job candidate is practicing better posture. Try marching in place to get into realignment. Or, pretend you are doing a marital art. If you are slumped over and your body resembles the letter "C," it's time to walk differently, talk differently, and stand tall.

INTENTION
Help me to straighten up both figuratively and literally. Give me a willing heart to move on with my life. Give me the courage to speak only kindness about myself and others. Amen!

ACTION
I promise if I can't say something nice, I will remain silent or focus on gratitude. I promise to practice stretching my hands over my head at least twice a day.

IDEA #34 CHANGE YOUR IMAGE: SAY NICE THINGS AND LOOK NICE, TOO

I promise if I can't say something nice, I will remain silent or focus on gratitude.
I promise to practice stretching my hands over my head at least twice a day.

IDEA #35

LOOK FOR THE GOOD
AND THEN LOOK AGAIN

IDEA #35 LOOK FOR THE GOOD AND THEN LOOK AGAIN

You know who they are. You know, the ones that hate their boss, they hate their job, they hate that they've been laid off. They can't find one good thing good to say about anything. Maybe you're that way. If you're job hunting and depressed, it's very easy to get in the "bitter" habit. Being bitter is a bad habit and will keep you from being hired. You cannot control what another person does, but you can control how you react. It's time to practice looking for the good.

There are few practical things you can do:

1. Stay away from other people who can't say anything nice either.
2. Journal. Commit to writing one unedited page a day. On paper vent, whine, write about nothing, or write about something. Just write, even if it means writing, "I don't feel like writing. I don't feel like writing. I don't feel like writing…"
3. Look for the good. Find three things a day of things that ARE going well. It's a spiritual discipline to find the good. It's like exercising a muscle that you haven't used for a long time. It may feel awkward at first, but after a few weeks, you'll get better at finding the good. It might be things like, "Well, at least I have food in my belly.". Or, "At least the sun didn't fall on me!"
4. Forgive the son of a #$@%&*. Or forgive the situation. It's okay to even forgive God. Forgiveness doesn't mean that you release the responsibility of the person, place, or situation from the harm caused. Forgiveness means you release the need to judge, condemn, or punish. By letting go of the emotional and physical charge, you will have more energy to job hunt.
5. Create a "Resentment is Poison" jar. There is a saying that resentment is like putting poison in your body and expecting the other person to die. Resentments hurt you. Resentments keep you from focusing on the constructive, positive steps to find work. Every time you get bitter and mad again, write what happened on a piece of paper and put it in your jar. If the same memory comes up and you get mad again, write what happened on a piece of paper and put it in your jar. Then at the end of 30 days, put all those little slips of paper in a blender. Add two cups of water and pulverize them! Or just throw them away.

You can see from these practical steps that there is a place for you to say something negative, just not to the people who may end up being an advocate for you.

INTENTION
Help me not to bad mouth anyone today. Help me to be kind. Let me focus on the good, even if it only lasts a few minutes. Help me be patient with myself as I try the practical steps to be better, not bitter. Thank you for listening. Amen!

ACTION
My promise is to be willing to forgive others and to embrace the champion who lives inside me.

IDEA #35 LOOK FOR THE GOOD AND THEN LOOK AGAIN

My promise is to be willing to forgive others and to embrace the champion who lives inside me.

Write down three good things:

I am grateful because…_____

I am grateful because…_____

I am grateful because…_____

Write down positive three things that are going well:

I have… _____

I have… _____

I have… _____

IDEA #36

MAYBE YOU'RE JUST BEING A TAD TOO CIVILIZED

IDEA #36 MAYBE YOU'RE JUST BEING A TAD TOO CIVILIZED

You have been working hard. You have been going to the library and the coffee shop. You have been learning about career research meetings, and advice and information meetings. You may have even ventured out to a networking event.

You were taught to be civilized. That means following the rules, but not at the expense of having fun. Sometimes we need to let off steam to get back on track. The trick is to do this in a way that isn't illegal or destructive to yourself or others.

In Jungian psychology, there is the wild man archetype and the wild woman archetype. These are the aspects of us that do outrageous things and at the same time validate our higher spiritual self. An example of a wild thing to do is to run around your house naked with feathers in your toes, screaming to the top of your voice, "I will get a job and I will have fun doing it! I will do one thing brave today!" (As if running around the house naked isn't brave). If you live with someone, it's advisable to warn them first.

Just for fun, pretend you are a rooster. Roosters get attention without being self-conscious. They beckon in the dawn. They crow without restraint. Maybe you'd rather howl at the moon, instead. Give yourself an hour break from your job search each day.

Play a little. Be wild!

INTENTION
Thank you for giving me the freedom to be wild from time to time. Help me to let go of the worry and fear for just a little while. Amen!

ACTION
I promise to do one wild thing to let off steam.

IDEA #36 MAYBE YOU'RE JUST BEING A TAD TOO CIVILIZED

I promise to do one wild thing to let off steam.
(Note: I am only endorsing outrageous wildness when it doesn't harm you or others. Have fun!)

Using the space above, draw a really bad picture of a rooster crowing as the sun rises. Here's mine:

IDEA #37

WHEN IS A JOB HUNT LIKE A DEER HUNT?

IDEA #37 WHEN IS A JOB HUNT LIKE A DEER HUNT? *

Let's say looking for work is like a deer hunt. Your "game" is to capture wonderful employment. If you have the right target, be sure you're not going after your game with a pellet gun. You have next to no chance of generating any interest with an "I want a job letter" if you are approaching a company without any knowledge of a job opening. If, on the other hand, you convert your efforts by sending a request for advice and information, you have a 50% chance of getting a positive response, even if you have no one introducing you into your target companies. This only works if you follow-up with a phone call, and ask to meet.

You have an 85% to 95% chance of getting a positive response if you send an "I seek advice and information" letter with a strong referral into the company, assuming you follow-up with a phone call and request to meet.

Three things usually happen when you send an "I want a job letter," even if you send 1,000 of them:
1. You follow-up and find there are no openings.
2. You follow-up and find they have openings that are not appropriate for you.
3. You compete with hundreds possibly thousands of job applicants that use the same ineffective approach.

None of these produces the desired results. How many rejection letters do you need to receive before you realize it is your approach, not you? If you are going to land the big game of employment, do not go back to what you know. A pellet gun will not work.

If the odds are stacked against you, doesn't it make sense to try a different approach? Unfortunately, job hunters lose precious time and money by hiring companies that promise to send out 1,000 letters to potential employers, and then nothing happens.

It can be hard to believe that the best way to find work is through career research meetings, advice and information meetings, and networking events. That's how you will match your abilities with what an employer wants. You'll need firsthand information about where you could make the best contribution. You want to be in control. The hunt is on. You are going to get the prize. But you have to have your sights on the right approach.

INTENTION
Help me set my sights on growing solid relationships based on how I can best be of service to a potential employer. Give me the patience to build a network of advocates. Amen!

ACTION
I promise to spend two hours a day developing a network of advocates and alliances.

* Rest assured that no actual deer were killed by using "Deer Hunt" as a metaphor. I used it more from a childhood song where initially some obstacle presents itself and the chorus is: Can't go around it, can't go over it, can't go under it, guess we'll just have to go through it.

IDEA #37 WHEN IS A JOB HUNT LIKE A DEER HUNT?

I promise to spend two hours a day developing a network of advocates and alliances.

What are three reasons someone would help you?

1. _____

_____

_____

2. _____

_____

_____

3. _____

_____

_____

Possible answers:
1. The person you are talking to who is now employed was out of work longer than you.
2. The person you are talking to believes in you.
3. The person you are talking to refers you to a job opening, you get hired, and it makes him/her look good!

IDEA #38

THE BASICS: BUILD A STRONG "NEXT" BUTTON

IDEA #38 THE BASICS: BUILD A STRONG "NEXT" BUTTON

Admit it. Sometimes it seems like your energy just drains out of you. One of the ways to conserve your energy is to know when to move on. This requires a strong NEXT button.

If you've been searching longer than 90 days, chances are you have called and re-called prospective sources to no avail, particularly if you've mailed a request for an advice and information meeting without a referral introduction. Here is my advice once you've made the initial approach. Call them every other day for a total of FIVE times. Then move on. No matter how hard you pan for gold, you cannot turn gravel into gold by sifting longer. You have taken action. Yet you cannot control if they call you back. But you can control saying, "NEXT!"

Believe it or not, NEXT is an accomplishment. Eliminating prospective sources that do not pan out is PROGRESS. Celebrate that and move on. If you are a discouraged job hunter, how do you sound optimistic when talking to another person? How do you leave an optimistic sounding phone message? Practice! Record yourself so you can listen and improve. But you CAN do this! Please reward yourself regardless of the result. This reward could be as simple as a walk around the block. Here is a script to help you either set an appointment or NEXT!

First phone call may sound like this:
Hi, this is Pat Patel. I'm following up regarding the email that I sent a few days ago. Please call me at (your phone number). I look forward to chatting with you briefly.

Second phone call:
Hi, Pat Patel again. It seems like you and I share this in common: (name it). I am calling to request a brief 20-minute meeting to exchange ideas about (name it). I can be reached at (phone number).

Third phone call:
Hi, Pat Patel. You must be very busy. Busy people are the very people that I need to talk to, and I promise to be brief. Please call me at (phone number).

Fourth and Fifth call (keep the frustration out of your voice, be light and friendly):
Hi, Pat Patel calling. As I said in my email, I am requesting a brief advice and information meeting. I need firsthand information from experts like you. I see our meeting as mutually beneficial, and I hope you agree. Please call me at (phone number).

INTENTION
Give me courage to follow-up by phone every other business day. Thank you for being at my side while I practice using a NEXT button. Amen!

ACTION
I promise to reward myself by taking action regardless of the result. My reward could be a walk to the park, a hot bath, or a well-deserved nap.

IDEA #38 THE BASICS: BUILD A STRONG "NEXT" BUTTON

I promise to reward myself by taking action regardless of the result. My reward could be a walk to the park, a hot bath, or a well-deserved nap.

Draw a picture of your "Next" button onto a 3 x 5 card. Take it with you; then use it!

IDEA #39

THE BASICS: BE PREPARED AND BE ON TIME

IDEA #39 THE BASICS: BE PREPARED AND BE ON TIME

It's been weeks and weeks and finally you get a second interview. You don't want to blow it. So, you spend four hours the night before reading their Annual Report, downloading articles in newspapers about them. You rehearse your answers to tough job interviewing questions. You look up at the clock and it's 2:00 in the morning. How did that happen? You were planning to go to bed at 11:00. The interview is at 9:00 a.m. Do you go to bed or just stay up? If you go to bed, will you be able to shut off the millions of details swirling in your head? If you stay up, will you be sharp enough to be enthusiastic about this opportunity?

Then the next day, you are en route when you realize you've forgotten the employer's phone number to let them know that you are running late. You arrive 15 minutes late. You didn't get the job. Before you label yourself with all sorts of self-contempt remarks, like you deliberately sabotaged this opportunity, let's figure out what happened. The concept of time sometimes does not correspond well for people who are depressed. How else would three days or even three weeks pass by with it feeling like three minutes?

If time is an abstract concept to you right now, work backwards from when you need to leave the house. Then lay out your clothes the night before. Make sure you know where your keys are before you go to bed. Then look inside your bi-fold notebook and check that you have extra copies of your resume, the questions you will ask, and the employer's contact information, including a phone number.

If you need to leave the house at 8:30 a.m. to be at your 9:00 a.m. appointment on time, give yourself an extra 20 minutes. That means leaving the house at 8:10 a.m. Draw a huge "X" over 8:30 a.m. so your brain gets: Must leave by 8:10. That means you must be out of bed by 6:45 a.m. to give yourself an hour to eat and dress. At 7:45, you now have 25 minutes left to leave the house. Don't get distracted. Leave the house by 8:10 even if you have one more thing to do. If you find yourself in the car at 8:00, leave anyway. Once you've arrived at your destination, assuming traffic was great, it should be 8:40. Use a few minutes to review your resume and the questions that you will ask them. If you are nervous, get out of the car and pace. Now set your phone alarm for 5 minutes just to make sure you do not lose track of time. When the phone alarm goes off, go in and announce yourself. Always arrive 15 minutes early. 15 minutes early is actually on time. Congratulations! You are on time for your 9:00 a.m. appointment. Now relax, breathe, and settle in.

INTENTION

Guide my actions to do what it takes to be on time even if time doesn't make much sense right now. Once I get there, let me to be of service to the person interviewing me. Amen!

ACTION

I promise to know where everything is the night before. I promise to work backwards to figure out what time I need to leave to arrive at my appointment 15 minutes early.

IDEA #39 THE BASICS: BE PREPARED AND BE ON TIME

I promise to know where everything is the night before. I promise to work backwards to figure out what time I need to leave to arrive at my appointment 15 minutes early.

Write about your relationship with time. Do you have an internal clock that's pretty accurate? Does the concept of time elude you? Are you late in order to feel bad about yourself? Are you late because you have no energy? Are you early because you feel better about yourself? Are you early to respect the other person's time? There are no right or wrong answers. Just notice your pattern.

_____

_____

_____

_____

_____

_____

_____

_____

_____

_____

_____

_____

_____

_____

_____

_____

_____

_____

_____

IDEA #40

WHAT, ME WORRY?
STOP THE "WHAT IF" GAME

IDEA #40 WHAT, ME WORRY? STOP THE "WHAT IF" GAME

Do you know what's worse than you worrying about getting a job? Answer: When your loved ones and friends worry about you getting a job. It's like a dog chasing his tail. Round and round the dog goes. It looks like productivity, but it's not. It's worry. Worry doesn't get you one day sooner or one day closer to the job you want to secure.

If worry doesn't get you what you want, why do you do it? There is a useful purpose to worry: It helps you figure out the worst-case scenario. How long will you live in a state of depression before you seek outside help? How long will you have to be out of work before you are homeless? How long will you have to be out of work before people give up on you? Or if you are working: How long will you have to stay in that "wrong fit" job before you make a positive change? Contingency planning is different than stirring up fear.

What if you are out of work three months, six months, a year? How are these questions helpful? The truth is you don't know if you are going to be homeless, exhausted, hospitalized, or abandoned. All you have are THESE 24 hours to get through. STOP scaring yourself with "What If" questions. Take a deep breath. Assume you will have all you need in these 24 hours.

Every time you start to worry, turn to the worry, acknowledge it, and say, "I know you are afraid. I am here for you. What can I do to help you be less afraid?" Every time you start to worry, say to yourself, "All I am doing is scaring myself. I know I'm making this disastrous scenario in my imagination. But NOTHING is happening NOW."

Worry can also be a sneaky way to not take responsibility for your Daily Action Plan (Refer back to IDEA #6). Watch how worry can completely stop you in your tracks. How then could anyone expect to hold you accountable to your overall job search action plan? Skip forward to IDEA #43 to give you something to do besides worry. If you grew up with worriers, worry can sometimes be mistaken for love. Because worry is a learned behavior, it can be unlearned (sometimes with professional help).

If you are going to make something up anyway, then make something up in your imagination where you are gainfully employed, appreciated, and back on track. Stay away from other "ain't-it-awful" people. STOP scaring yourself with negative "what ifs." Instead, imagine that you are in perfect health and in the perfect job at the perfect time.

INTENTION
Just for these 24 hours, help me practice imagining a positive future. Guide me to a better way of thinking so I can escape the trap of worrying. Amen!

ACTION
My promise is to gently remind myself that just for today, I have all I need. My promise today is to breathe and relax as I throw away worry like yesterday's newspaper.

IDEA #40 WHAT, ME WORRY? STOP THE "WHAT IF" GAME

My promise is to gently remind myself that just for today, I have all I need.

My promise today is to breathe and relax as I throw away worry like yesterday's newspaper.

Draw a picture of a dog chasing its tail. Name the dog "Worry."

Now draw a picture of a dog on a leash heading in the right direction. Name this dog "Determination."

IDEA #41

THE BASICS: THE PHONE INTERVIEW: THE FIRST BIG HURDLE

IDEA #41 THE BASICS: THE PHONE INTERVIEW: THE FIRST BIG HURDLE

More and more companies are using the telephone for the first job interview. It saves time. The interviewer will seldom spend more than 15 to 25 minutes on the phone. This first interview is used more to screen you out more than to screen you in. That's a lot of pressure! Yet there are things you can do to increase your chances.

First, dress as if they can see you. Put on your best business attire. Why? Because it's difficult to feel powerful in your pajamas and uncombed hair.

Secondly, do something that will make you feel powerful. Try standing during the entire phone interview. One person said to me, "Well at least I was taller than they were!" Another person I know always did 20 jumping jacks five minutes before the call, just to get the blood flowing.

Thirdly, be prepared. Have a list of questions you want to ask them. Create a checklist of what you want to say. Have the research on the company handy and highlighted in yellow. Minimize distractions. Turn off the television, the radio, and ask a neighbor to watch your loud and unpredictable children or pets. Last, but not least, smile. Because you cannot be seen during a phone interview, you need to compensate for that disadvantage. Your voice should convey confidence, friendliness, and warmth.

Sometimes imagining that the job interviewer is holding your favorite pet can ease the pressure you feel. Sometimes imagining the job interviewer smiling back can put you at ease. Sometimes by reminding yourself that your focus is on the job interviewer's needs and NOT on self-monitoring your performance, will help. Regardless of what you do to prepare, relax as best as you can. Even though the job interviewer will be asking about your competencies, they are really evaluating compatibility and if the chemistry is right for them to bring you in for a face-to-face interview.

INTENTION
Help me to set aside my worry about how I will perform during my first phone interview. Give me the confidence to relax, smile, and answer the questions to the best of my abilities. Amen!

ACTION
I promise to practice phone interviews with others so when the real one happens I will be confident and prepared.

IDEA #41 THE BASICS: THE PHONE INTERVIEW: THE FIRST BIG HURDLE

I promise to practice phone interviews with others so when the real one happens

I will be confident and prepared.

Write a few lines about how you will stay calm and focused during the interview.

_____

_____

_____

_____

_____

_____

_____

_____

_____

_____

_____

_____

_____

_____

_____

_____

_____

_____

_____

IDEA #42

THE BASICS:
SALARY NEGOTIATION BEGINS
DURING THE VERY FIRST INTERVIEW

IDEA #42 THE BASICS:
SALARY NEGOTIATION BEGINS DURING THE VERY FIRST INTERVIEW

The purpose of the first interview is to get the second interview. The purpose of the second interview is to get the third interview. Part of how you accomplish that is to not talk about money until there is a job offer. Questions about your salary history and your salary expectations are designed to screen you out. Don't do it! This is difficult because you will always be asked. It's awkward not to answer, but with practice, you can be an artful dodger (in the good sense). There are hundreds of job interviewing questions and some books give you sample questions with sample answers. But if the sample answers don't sound like you, do not use words and phrases that do not match up to the way you talk. It all boils down to five guiding principles.

1. Use all questions to showcase your talents and interests.
2. Do not bad mouth yourself or others, particularly a former boss.
3. Do not assume the question being asked is appropriate or worth answering.
4. When in doubt, answer the question with a question. It is okay to clarify.
5. Do not talk about your salary history or salary expectations until there is a job offer.

There are standard questions that are always asked, most frequently: "Tell me about yourself." Give a brief summary of your background with three skills that you enjoy using. Use diplomacy and discretion when you are asked about the worst boss you ever had. Be kind to the interviewer if they ask a stupid question. This is a great time to answer the question with a question such as "Could you help me understand why this is important to you?"
www.CourageousChange.net

If you are asked a question that you don't want to answer, try using softening language like, "If you don't mind.....or I was wondering....or I am curious....." This helps deflect the awkwardness of you not answering the question.

For instance, "I am curious why you need to know that information?" or "If you don't mind, I'd like to delay talking about money until we determine that we are a good fit for each other." When asked about your salary expectations, you could answer, "I'm sure you have a range in mind, what is the range for this position?"

If the first couple of interviews are conducted by someone other than the department head, keep in mind that your job is to make the interviewer look good. Otherwise, why would the interviewer risk recommending you to the decision maker? Keep in mind that job interviewing is a two way street. They are evaluating if you are a good fit and you are sizing them up, too. Job interviewing is about developing a new relationship. That means your approach should feel more like peer-to-peer than thinking they have power over you.

INTENTION
God, if I thought about You being my employer, then maybe that would help take the pressure off. Help me be of service to the job interviewer, even if they don't hire me. Amen!

ACTION
I promise to memorize the five job interviewing principles and keep my mouth shut about money, even though they will ask, and ask again.

IDEA #42 THE BASICS: SALARY NEGOTIATION BEGINS DURING THE VERY FIRST INTERVIEW

I promise to memorize the five job interviewing principles and keep my mouth shut about money, even though they will ask, and ask again.

Write three reasons why you WOULD negotiate for more money when the offer comes in.

_____

_____

_____

_____

_____

_____

_____

_____

_____

_____

_____

Write three reasons why you would NOT negotiate for more money when the offer comes in.

_____

_____

_____

_____

_____

_____

_____

_____

_____

_____

_____

IDEA #43

THE BASICS: FOLLOW THE SCENT –
HOW TO MEASURE FORWARD PROGRESS

IDEA #43 THE BASICS:
FOLLOW THE SCENT – HOW TO MEASURE FORWARD PROGRESS

You will need four tools to find work:
1. A Focus
2. A Plan
3. Accountability
4. Measurable Success Actions.

If you have the wrong plan, or the wrong focus, or the wrong action, who is going to tell you? Choosing a sounding board will help you get clear about whether or not you are moving in the right direction. Yet for some of you, getting clear is about taking action first. I call this the following-the-scent approach. You get a whiff of something that sounds appealing and you seek it out. That's okay, too. Consider using a career coach to help you not go off base.

If you say to yourself I'm not that organized, chances are what would work best for you is to measure forward progress by Units of activity rather than using a predictable schedule. You might commit to doing one thing a day toward your job search no matter what. When you are ready to do more, then do three or more units a day. Job search units [of activity] are not tied to time; they are tied into how many units you are willing to consistently do each day.

Once you start, don't stop. Don't ask me why, but it's been my experience that if you shut your job search down a week, it takes three weeks to build momentum back to where you were before.

If you do view yourself as an organized person, then try using Time to measure your efforts. Decide how much time you can spend on your job search and create a predictable routine. It might be Mon-

day, coffee shop; Tuesday, library; Wednesday and Thursday, career research meetings.

Staying on track is what accountability is all about. If you aren't finding work when you thought you would, evaluate how you are spending your time. It is really easy to think you are job hunting, when in fact all you are doing is thinking about it. Take a thorough look at what action you are taking to make sure your plan is on target. If you said you would talk to one person a day about your job search, and you find yourself reverting back to only searching for work online, you will notice you are off track faster when you have a way to measure your forward progress.

Finding work is the ultimate in delayed gratification. That's why Success Metrics are so important. When you take action, reward yourself along the way. Holding yourself accountable isn't always glamorous or fun, but it will strengthen your forward movement. Reward yourself for keeping your commitments, not your results.

INTENTION
Thank you for giving me a way to pay attention to what I am doing with my job search plan. Give me the strength to take action each day, and then reward myself for doing what I said I would. Amen!

ACTION
My promise is to follow the scent when something appeals to me. My promise is to do one thing each day related to my job search and/or create a predictable routine measured by time.

IDEA #43 THE BASICS: FOLLOW THE SCENT – HOW TO MEASURE FORWARD PROGRESS

My promise is to follow the scent when something appeals to me. My promise is to do one thing each day related to my job search and/or create a predictable routine measured by time.

Make a list of Weekly Job Search activities, and decide how much you will do.

1 Trip to the library for research

1 Research session using bizjournals.com or other newspaper sites

1 Networking or business event

10 Email letters (requests for informational meetings, fan letters, and follow-up updates)

10 Phone calls

3 Career research or informational meetings (this is what builds momentum in your search)

3 Thank you letters

5 Follow-up calls four weeks after informational meetings to give progress updates

5 Applying for jobs online

1 Job interview (this takes a while to build up to this)

IDEA #44

IS YOUR DOGGIE DOOR ATS (APPLICANT TRACKING SYSTEM) COMPLIANT?

IDEA #44 IS YOUR DOGGIE DOOR ATS (APPLICANT TRACKING SYSTEM) COMPLIANT?

Find a door within the interior of your home. Your front door will do. Allow your hand to touch the entire door from top to bottom. Now imagine that this door, top to bottom, represents the entirety of every opportunity that is waiting for you. Let yourself imagine that at the bottom of the door is a doggie door big enough for a Pug to go through. For the sake of this exercise, that doggie door represents ALL the opportunity you can find online, through company websites and recruiters. I bet most of you would be too big to crawl through. Next, imagine you have figured out a way to make that doggie door big enough for a Saint Bernard to go through. Could you crawl through now? For most of you the answer would be "Yes."

Why make the doggie door bigger? Remember even though the doggie door only represents advertised opportunities, it shouldn't be ignored. Yet if that expanded doggie door represents 25% of all opportunities, then plan to spend 25% of your job search time looking for advertised positions. How did you get it to Saint Bernard size? Two ways: through making your resume ATS (Applicant Tracking System) compatible and by building a strong LinkedIn presence.

Let's start with the ATS. This is a software program that seamlessly scans applicant resumes and analyzes how many keywords match the description of the job posting. Imagine ATS as a little robot that decides if you get screened in or screened out. This saves Human Resources lots of time by only selecting candidates whose resumes match what they are looking for. The disadvantage to you is that you could have been the best candidate for the job but because you might have failed to insert their keywords, that little robot didn't screen you in. Good news! That's fixable. There are many companies that sell ATS software and you do not need to know how each of them work. I would suggest though, downloading 6 to 10 job descriptions, print them off, and use a yellow highlighter to see how many phrases and words repeat. You can also copy and paste those job descriptions into a single Word document, and use the "find and select" feature to count the frequency. Then analyze if those phrases or words are in your resume. YouTube is an excellent resource to learn more about ATS. My colleague Joanne Meehl has an excellent video that further explains it. Just type into YouTube's search feature "ATS Joanne Meehl" and you will find it right away. If for any reason, it's not there, then just type in "ATS" or "Applicant Tracking System". I'll explain LinkedIn on a separate page, but know that the more keywords you have in your LinkedIn profile, the more likely you will be found there, too.

INTENTION

Thank you for giving me the ability to learn new things about how to get the Applicant Tracking System software to screen me in. Amen!

ACTION

I promise to watch 3 YouTube videos about ATS (Applicant Tracking System), and then analyze how many new words or phrases I need to add to my resume to increase my odds of being screened in.

IDEA #44 IS YOUR DOGGIE DOOR ATS (APPLICANT TRACKING SYSTEM) COMPLIANT?

I promise to watch 3 YouTube videos about ATS (Applicant Tracking System), and then analyze how many new words or phrases I need to add to my resume to increase my odds of being screened in.

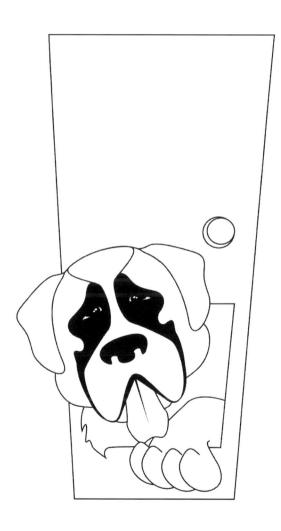

IDEA #45
THE POWER OF LINKEDIN

IDEA #45 THE POWER OF LINKEDIN

If you haven't job searched for more than five years, then you probably missed the explosion of influence that www.LinkedIn.com has become. The trend is if you do not have a LinkedIn presence, more and more employers won't even consider you. To make matters worse, if you do have a LinkedIn presence, but have less than 50 people connected to your profile, you will not be at the top of the recruiter's list. At this point, you may find yourself panicking because you only know 20 people. That's okay. Invite those 20 people to connect to you on LinkedIn anyway. Eventually, you will develop strategies to expand your LinkedIn community.

Let's start with the basics. What is LinkedIn? LinkedIn is a social media site for the business and non-profit community. It's free to use. You do not need to purchase the premium account. LinkedIn is relatively spam proof because you only accept people you know to connect to you. It is not there for you to post cute puppies. Rather, LinkedIn is like your professional website, and you get to build it for free. Think of LinkedIn like a business card with power. You get to say who you are and what you want to attract. The more LinkedIn connections you have, the larger your searchable database becomes, which makes it more likely you will be found by recruiters and / or the more likely you are to find like-minded employers. It's all based on algorithms and you will use the advanced search feature by learning a process called the Boolean search. Type in "Boolean search recruiting" in any search engine to learn more.

LinkedIn is a powerful research tool to help you prepare for job interviews. With a large enough connection base (usually 100 people or more), you can actually research and talk to people who work at your target companies and /or the same occupations you want to research. You can get the insider scoop and prepare better questions for the interview as a result of your research.

There are hundreds of pages written about LinkedIn online, as well as books to buy, and YouTube videos to review. Your competition is using LinkedIn, and so should you. Be curious about LinkedIn and use it at least once a week. In addition to the LinkedIn community, you can participate in free LinkedIn specialty groups. This will give you increased visibility if you comment on articles that were posted within the group. Always keep your comments constructive and respectful. You are creating a positive image for others to see.

More and more employers are reviewing your LinkedIn profile before they decide if they want to bring you in for an interview. There is also a job postings feature on LinkedIn. Work with others to make sure your profile is free from spelling errors or a lousy photo or content that speaks poorly about you and your job search. Work with a career coach, like me, who stays current in how LinkedIn changes and how you can adapt. The goal is to create a compelling story about your work experience and your positive future.

INTENTION

Thank you for giving me a mind to learn new things. Give me the patience and confidence to improve my LinkedIn profile. Amen!

ACTION

Just for today, I will learn as much as I can about LinkedIn profiles, review the profiles of others, and evaluate how to make mine better.

IDEA #45 THE POWER OF LINKEDIN

Just for today, I will learn as much as I can about LinkedIn profiles, review the profiles of others, and evaluate how to make mine better.

IDEA #46
AND NOW FOR THE UNWANTED ATTENTION

IDEA #46 AND NOW FOR THE UNWANTED ATTENTION

You spend months and months being rejected or worse yet ignored, and then you post your resume to a job board like www.indeed.com and suddenly you get unwanted attention. Some are like flying gnats and some are darn right scammers trying to lure you into making some quick cash and you end up being taken to the cleaners. The bottom line is if it sounds too good to be true, it probably is.

Let's start with people who find your resume online and want you to be part of their network marketing team, sometimes called MLM (multi-level marketing). If you haven't had any interviews, this can initially be very attractive to you. It is an opportunity for you to be your own business owner with very little investment on your part. Many of these businesses have great reputations and then there are those that promise you the moon and deliver next to nothing. One now defunct MLM travel business required my client to pay $50 a month for her personal website and after 6 months my client made a total of $10. That's a $290 loss not to mention the time and energy wasted. Any legitimate network marketing business doesn't promise big bucks. Instead, they promise limited revenues (initially under $500 a month) that can grow over time. If you have been out of work so long you are about to lose your house, I do not recommend MLM as your solution. They take a lot of time and energy to develop, and you will want a quicker income generator.

Also, don't be surprised if multiple insurance companies try to recruit you. This can be initially flattering, particularly if no one else is calling. Insurance is a tough business, involving long hours, and lots of rejection. This line of work is not for the faint of heart. Usually a straight commission job, it takes about 6 months or longer for

decent revenues to start coming in. That means YOU have to pay out of your own savings while you build your book of business. There is high turnover in the insurance industry, which is why they recruit out-of-work people so aggressively. If you choose to go into insurance (or any other straight commission opportunity) be sure to be willing to expend at least 6 months of your cash reserves or negotiate with your partner at home to support you while you get established.

Last are the people who contact you that should be thrown in jail. They use the seduction of hope and appeal to your greed and ask you to buy into a scheme that will make you a lot of money. Most of the time they require a "processing fee" or an "application fee" ranging from $100 to $500 in return for supposed access to an exclusive offer where you will make over $10,000. These scams vary. One job candidate I know paid for a background check that cost him $250 so he could transport cars across multiple states with the promise to make $2,000. It was a fake opportunity and he lost the money with nothing to show for it. Buyer beware. Yet do not ignore job boards just because you want to avoid unwanted attention. It's just the road noise you have to put up with to find more attractive job opportunities. Sort through what won't work and focus on what will.

INTENTION
Thank you for giving me the patience to sort through what opportunities will work for me and just ignore the rest. Amen!

ACTION
When I am online, I promise to only focus on opportunities that make sense and not get distracted by the ones that won't pay me money.

IDEA #46 AND NOW FOR THE UNWANTED ATTENTION

When I am online, I promise to only focus on opportunities that make sense and not get distracted by the ones that won't pay me money.

IDEA #47

SWITCH!

IDEA #47 SWITCH!

I had planned on sleeping an extra hour when suddenly my mind started adding numbers together. The more I added, the more awake I became. I asked myself what was I doing adding numbers when my job at that moment was to be sleeping and replenishing. "SWITCH" is a command you will be saying loudly and firmly when your mind starts wandering away from the task at hand. If you have the same kind of busy mind I have, you will be saying it frequently. Here are some things your mind might say as you change the way you think, feel, and act on your job search:

I will never find work. SWITCH!

I always find dead-end jobs. SWITCH!

Nobody appreciates me. SWITCH!

I'm too tired to do anything today. SWITCH!

That employer didn't call me back for a second interview because I'm no good. SWITCH!

I might as well be dead. SWITCH!

No one understands what I am going through. SWITCH!

I won't do information meetings because.... SWITCH!

These thoughts are like big boulders that block your way to the road of your job search success. When you say "SWITCH!" these thoughts can disappear like vapor (with practice). Thoughts drive feelings, and when you change your nasty thoughts by saying, "SWITCH!" you have an opportunity to ask yourself, "What feeling is underneath that thought?" What if feelings and thoughts really don't matter? What if what really matters is you taking positive action? Remember in the first idea? Eeyore didn't fundamentally change his state of mind throughout all the tales of Winnie the Pooh. He was still one depressed donkey. Yet he succeeded because he took action and had the support of others along the way. You can do that, too. You have the power to change the channel just like when you switch the channel when watching television. Don't like the program you are watching? Switch the channel. Take a walk, call a friend, or go to a coffee shop. SWITCH! And yes, there may be times when outside professional help such as psychotherapy may be the only way to SWITCH! And if that's the case, do it! No excuses.

INTENTION
Protect me from my busy mind, particularly when my mind says abusive things to me like I am no good. Help me strengthen my ability to say "SWITCH" and then develop strategies to compensate for managing those nasty thoughts. Amen!

ACTION
Just for today, I will practice saying "SWITCH" when a negative thought tries to get me off track.

IDEA #47 SWITCH!

Just for today, I will practice saying, "SWITCH" when a negative thought tries to get me off track.

Sometimes negative thinking is just a bad habit, yet without examining the underlying assumptions, you might assume what you are thinking is true. Look at these four columns.

Assumption	If That's True I Can...	Counter Statement	If That's True I Can...
I will never find work.	Just give up.	I haven't found work yet.	Do three things today on my job search list.
I always find dead-end jobs.	Feel sorry for myself.	I am willing to find work that offers career advancement.	Research and find companies that promote from within. Target them.
I will never find work.	I will sell my house to have money to live on.	I will keep looking until I find the right job for me.	Trust that the action I take today will lead to success.
Nobody appreciates me.	Eat a quart of ice cream to comfort myself.	I am grateful for what I have.	Ask for what I want

IDEA #48

WHEN ALL ELSE FAILS, SAY "THANK YOU!"

IDEA #48 WHEN ALL ELSE FAILS, SAY "THANK YOU!"

Thank each person who has helped you along the way, and them thank them again once you have found work. I remember working with a large corporation that unexpectedly fired several professionals. I was faced with the difficult task of creating an atmosphere of hope while giving participants an opportunity to vent about their unexpected job loss. When people are traumatized by the rug being pulled out from under them, their capacity to listen and learn about the career transition process is always compromised. Yet when hope is restored, learning does occur, and then I never hear from these participants again. That was the case for this particular project except for Mr. Adams.

Mr. Adams wrote me a letter thanking me for restoring his hope. He told me I had helped him face the daunting task of grieving the loss of a job he loved and sorting out the complexities of a job search. My presentation gave him a framework to get back on his feet and make a successful career move. Actually, what really happened was I gave him an invitation to move forward. He accepted and took action. Over the years, he repaid my kindness over and over again. We developed a powerful, mutually beneficial relationship for many years. That power was gratitude.

You, too, can create a deeper impression on those you influence through the power of gratitude. Whether it's the first interview, the second or the third, always send a heartfelt thank you note. Whether it's a five-minute exchange at a networking event or an hour-long networking meeting, you will be remembered longer if you send a thank you note. Why? Because, so few people do it!

Send a thank you to those who helped you after you have made a successful career transition. Sadly, many people start their jobs and never acknowledge the many people who took the time to help. It's an easy thing to forget after the exhaustion of a search and the busyness of a new job. Yet those who do send thank you notes will have an easier time with their next career campaign two years, three years, five years down the road. Think about it. If you re-activate your search and you try to reconnect with someone who never heard what happened to you, do you truly think they will be as willing to help you as readily the second time around?

A successful career transition requires a commitment to be in your life differently. I remember a client who even sent a thank you note for being turned down for a job he really wanted. His note was so compelling that the company expanded the finalist list from three to four, and suddenly he was back in the race. His thank you turned the tide; he was hired! You, too, will feel more in control when you practice daily gratitude.

INTENTION
Help me practice gratitude when I wake up and each evening before I go to bed at night. Amen!

ACTION
I promise to keep a daily gratitude journal to remember that I have all I need. Then when I have a particularly bad day, I will open my gratitude journal to remind myself that better days are coming.

IDEA #48 WHEN ALL ELSE FAILS, SAY "THANK YOU!"

I promise to keep a daily gratitude journal to remember that just for today I have all I need. Then when I have a particularly bad day, I will open my gratitude journal to remind myself that better days are coming.

Thank you for..._____

Thank you for..._____

Thank you for... _____

IDEA #49

DON'T GIVE UP BEFORE THE MIRACLE HAPPENS

IDEA #49 DON'T GIVE UP BEFORE THE MIRACLE HAPPENS

What if you are doing everything right and still have not achieved the result you want after four months? Keep going! What if you are doing everything right and you still haven't achieved the result you want after eight months? Keep going! Don't give up before the miracle happens. Remember: Chin Up, Chin Out, and Go!

Every six weeks, analyze your activity. Did you invest ten hours a week consistently? Did you do three things a day from your job search plan? Have you been willing to do advice and information meetings, and career research meetings? Have you been willing to attend free networking events? Have you stayed away from online applications until after 3:00 p.m.?

Are you getting enough sleep? Are you taking walks? Are you making mistakes and then correcting them so they don't get in the way the next time around? Have you given yourself permission to be imperfect? Keep going!

Something miraculous happens when your actions hit critical mass. Some call it a tipping point. Suddenly without any additional effort on your part, the phone rings, you get called in for an interview, then you get called in for another interview from a different company, and you receive two offers in the same week. Don't stop until that miracle happens for you.

Something happens when you realize momentum has picked up, and suddenly your advice and information meetings are paying off. You have the amazing problem of having so many referrals you can't get to all of them. Now you have to set priorities about whether you can get to them in ten days or six weeks. Don't stop until that miracle happens for you.

If this hasn't happened for you yet, keep going! Read, learn, and apply job search ideas. Now is the time to stay in action, to re-read this book, and to continue to get positive and constructive support from others.

INTENTION
Guide my actions to do what it takes to keep going. Give me the strength to keep going, even when I am not seeing results. Help me trust that momentum will pick up as long as I keep taking action. Amen!

ACTION
I promise to keep going until I hear those wonderful words: "Welcome aboard!"

IDEA #49 DON'T GIVE UP BEFORE THE MIRACLE HAPPENS

I promise to keep going until I hear those wonderful words: "Welcome aboard!"

Draw a picture of what "WELCOME ABOARD" looks like. Imagine celebrating your great, new job!

THE PROMISES OF ACTION

1. I will take one positive action, even if it means just getting out of bed.
2. I will take one positive step to honor my losses. I will make a list of all my losses on different pieces of toilet paper. When it is time, I will flush this list down the toilet, and let my losses go.
3. I will do one thing from my self-care list, and then do one more. But first, I will get out of bed.
4. I will experiment with doing THREE fun things today, then and only then, do ONE job search activity.
5. I will pay attention to how I spend my time, and let go of the activities that just numb me out.
6. I will wait to apply for jobs online until after 3:00 p.m. My promise is to get out of bed, get dressed as if I were going to work, and then leave the house even if it means driving around the block and coming back home.
7. I will make a plan to protect myself from negative people. My promise is to get out of bed, get dressed, leave the house, and start looking for positive people.
8. I will breathe and relax as I create my inspiring job search headquarters.
9. I will read an inspiring book or watch an inspiring movie where the hero comes from behind and wins. My promise is to make mistakes and try again.
10. I will prepare a summary of the positive aspects of who I am and what I enjoy doing. Then I promise to rehearse my powerful story until it becomes second nature to me.
11. I will reach out to others to encourage me and hold me accountable.
12. I will train my loved ones to only ask me if I am keeping my promises. I will reassure them that I have a plan and am moving forward.
13. I will utilize time as a resource to get my job search plan in place.
14. I will pay attention to possible dream jobs. I promise to write down and acknowledge that inside those ideas are important clues about what I want to do.
15. I will learn more about what occupations might be a good fit for me. I promise to be open to a better life and explore occupations that work for me.
16. I will face my fears and let them pass through. I promise to relax as I learn new things.
17. I will make a list of 20 things that personally interest (or used to interest me). I will choose my top five to match similar industries and markets.
18. I will go to a bookstore to see how topics are organized. I promise to go to the library and learn how organizations are classified.
19. I will select organizations that I will put on my target list.
20. I will buy a journal and write in it daily.
21. I will breathe and relax as I build my workable information retrieval system.
22. I will look inside and find specific examples of my natural abilities.

23. I will see myself with assets and deficits, a beautiful weaving of being uniquely human. My promise is to be willing to be of service to a future employer.

24. I will think through what I want my career research project to be.

25. I will make a list of people I want to contact first, second, and third. I will share my Career Research Ideas document with people who are likely to introduce me to others.

26. I will let one person know who I am, and what I am exploring, and ask for referrals. Then I will do it again. I will practice with people who are not threatening to me.

27. I will find ten people, even if they are strangers, and practice my script. I will have paper and pen with me, so when I get real introductions I will be able to write them down.

28. I will find an article in a Business Journal or newspaper that is about one of my target markets. Just for fun, I will write a letter to the author of the article or a contact person mentioned in the article. Then I promise to follow-up by phone and ask to meet.

29. I will expand my knowledge about my target markets even when I am in the practice stage of Advice and Information meetings.

30. I will write my top 7 to 12 questions I will ask in an Advice and Information meeting.

31. I will become better known and tell others about what I am targeting. If any day gets too overwhelming, my promise is to go to a coffee shop and talk to one person anyway.

32. I will practice how to work a room.

33. I will go to the library and check out two books on how to write a resume.

34. I promise if I can't say something nice, I will remain silent or focus on gratitude. I promise to practice stretching my hands over my head at least twice a day.

35. My promise is to be willing to forgive others and to embrace the champion who lives inside me.

36. I will do one wild thing to let off steam.

37. I will spend two hours a day developing a network of advocates and alliances.

38. I will reward myself by taking action regardless of the result. My reward could be a walk to the park, a hot bath, or a well-deserved nap.

39. I promise to know where everything is the night before. I promise to work backwards to figure out what time I need to leave to arrive at my appointment 15 minutes early.

40. I will gently remind myself that just for today, I have all I need. My promise today is to breathe and relax as I throw away worry like yesterday's newspaper.

41. I will practice phone interviews with others so when the real one happens I will be confident and prepared.

42. I will memorize the five job interviewing principles and keep my mouth shut about money, even though they will ask, and ask again.

43. My promise is to follow the scent when something appeals to me. My promise is to do one thing each day related to my job search and/ or create a predictable routine measured by time.

44. I will watch three YouTube videos about ATS (Applicant Tracking System), and then analyze how many new words or phrases I need to add to my resume to increase my odds of being screened in.

45. I will learn as much as I can about LinkedIn profiles, will review the profiles of others, and evaluate how to make mine better.

46. I will focus only on online opportunities that make sense and not get distracted by the ones that won't pay me money.

47. I will practice saying "SWITCH" when a negative thought tries to get me off track.

48. I will keep a daily gratitude journal to remember that I have all I need. Then when I have a particularly bad day, I will open my gratitude journal to remind myself that better days are coming.

49. I promise to keep going until I hear those wonderful words: "Welcome aboard!"

THE PRAYER INTENTIONS – "MAY IT BE SO!"

1. Help me to accept my current situation exactly the way it is. Help me to know that it's okay to be me, whether I am Pooh, or Tigger, or Piglet, or Eeyore. Give me the energy to find a Job Search Support Group or a trusted friend that will be part of this career transition experience. Thank you, for your support. God are greater than my current situation. Amen!

2. Comfort me when I do not feel in control of my own destiny. Help me grieve and let go of my losses. Amen!

3. Thank you for reminding me that being overwhelmed is a normal part of change. Help me to remember to start each day with self-care first. Amen!

4. Thank you for giving me permission to have fun, fun, fun, and then work...well at least in the short run. Thank you for giving me permission to relax as part of my job search plan. With your help, I'll keep taking action and leaving the results to you. Amen!

5. Help me to remember that "GOD" stands for Good Orderly Direction. Give me the strength to do the next right thing. Help me to put one foot in front of the other, each and every day. Help me to organize my day so it is filled with life and productivity and fun. Thank you for giving me a mind that works, at least some of the time. Amen!

6. Give me the willingness to be open to new ways of job searching. Guide my actions so my energy will be restored. Give me the courage to write a Daily Action Plan and then do it. Amen!

7. Protect me from negative people. Guide my actions so that my energy will be restored. Give me the courage to stay away from people who deplete me. Amen!

8. If I build it, will they come? Help me to create a place just for my job search to take myself seriously. Guide my preparations so that when I sit down to go to work, I'm ready. Thank you for giving me the willingness to get ready. Amen!

9. Guide my actions so that my confidence will be restored. Give me the courage to look inside and find the good. Help me to get ready to take stock of my life. Amen!

10. Thank you for giving me the words that tell my story. Give me the courage to start telling my positive story to others who can help me. Amen!

11. Help me to not overuse my loved ones for venting and complaining. Thank you for bringing people into my life who will be part of my success team. I can go home at night with my head held high, and really be there for my loved ones. Amen!

12. Thank you, God for the opportunity to have mutual support in my life. I know I've been isolating and staying away from well-meaning friends. Help me to reach out to them and ask them for support. Help me to write a letter to the ones I've driven away and let them know that I am sorry. Let me write and request what I need if I don't have the energy to verbally ask. Protect me and comfort me if they don't respond the way I want. Amen!

13. Thank you for giving me hope that I can take action even if I am still discouraged. Thank you for giving me permission to take it slowly. Guide my actions today and give me a willingness to change. Amen!

14. God, I want to dream about fun jobs. Help me to relax as I create structure for my job search. Help me to rest when I need to rest and take action when I need to take action. Help me to trust that once my job search routine is established that I will feel more competent again. In the meantime, thank you for giving me permission to dream. Amen!

15. Help me to be willing to believe that there is something better for me occupationally. Help me to trust that answers will come, even when I doubt. Thank you for giving me the energy to learn more about what occupations would be a better fit. Amen!

16. Guide my steps today. Give me courage to journal, to walk, and to learn other ways to job search. Thank you for giving me options for focusing on radical self-care. Amen!

17. Thank you for giving me a brain that works even when I am feeling pessimistic. Give me the patience to figure this out; trusting that if I do this step, my job search will be shortened. Thinking about industries and market sectors that match up to my interests is new to me. Help me accept the challenge to think about both my limits and my potential. Amen!

18. Thank you for giving me a mind to think and a mind to choose. Remind me that I have options, even when my negative thinking tells me I don't. With your help, I will act as if this preparation will get my job search going in the right direction. Amen!

19. Guide my actions today as I give myself permission to explore. Let me remember that this is just a starting point, subject to change. Help me to think of this as a field trip where I can learn and decide what organizations are right for me. Amen!

20. Help me to keep my promises today. Let me focus more on what I can control and less on what I can't. Thank you for the opportunity to write down my feelings, successes, mistakes, and my dreams. Amen!

21. Help me to put together an information retrieval system that is easy for me to use. Give me strength to be willing to put things away so I can find them later. Give me strength to be willing to actually talk to people I may not know. Amen!

22. Guide my memory to help me to write down five or more stories that can serve as proof of my abilities. Give me the courage to look inside by completing this phrase: "I remember a time when I...." Give me a quiet heart to remember times that I enjoyed. Let me be open to surrounding myself with a support team to remind me of who I am. Amen!

23. Let me believe that I can turn around my current job search. Guide my actions, as I give myself permission to approach the job market in a different way. Amen!

24. Let me be willing to try career research meetings. Guide my actions, as I give myself permission to approach the job market in a different way. Amen!

25. Give me the courage to become known to others. Amen!

26. Give me the courage to come out of hiding. Give me the strength to practice saying aloud what I want to do and what organizations I'd like to learn more about. Amen!

27. Thank you for giving me the tools to reach out to more people. Help me to understand I do not have to do it perfectly. Guide my actions so that I stop being the best kept secret around! Amen.

28. Give me the courage to risk writing to a total stranger. If I feel unworthy, let me ask anyway. Let me ask, even if the person I ask might say "No." Amen!

29. Let me be willing to add Advice and Information meetings to my job search plan. Guide my actions as I approach my job search in a different way. Amen!

30. Help me to imagine that I can be in the driver's seat. Give me the wisdom to become better known through Advice and Information meetings. Amen!

31. Help me to overcome any reluctance to networking. Guide my actions so that I may be of service to others, even when I'm down. Be with me, when I send that letter, when I follow-up, when I set the appointment, and when I actually leave the house and meet someone. Protect me from feelings of defeat if the meeting didn't go as planned. Amen!

32. Thank you for giving me hope that I can interact with more people. Guide my actions today and give me a willingness to change. Amen!

33. Help me to not get bogged down in creating the perfect resume. Guide my efforts to create an excellent resume. Help me find three people to check for spelling and grammatical errors before I send it out. Amen!

34. Help me to straighten up both figuratively and literally. Give me a willing heart to move on with my life. Give me the courage to speak only kindness about myself and others. Amen!

35. Help me not to bad mouth anyone today. Help me to be kind. Let me focus on the good, even if it only lasts a few minutes. Help me be patient with myself as I try the practical steps to be better, not bitter. Thank you for listening. Amen!

36. Thank you for giving me the freedom to be wild from time to time. Help me to let go of the worry and fear for just a little while. Amen!

37. Help me set my sights on growing solid relationships based on how I can best be of service to a potential employer. Give me the patience to build a network of advocates. Amen!

38. Give me courage to follow-up by phone every other business day. Thank you for being at my side while I practice using a NEXT button. Amen!

39. Guide my actions to do what it takes to be on time even if time doesn't make much sense right now. Once I get there, let me to be of service to the person interviewing me. Amen!

40. Just for these 24 hours, help me practice imagining a positive future. Guide me to a better way of thinking so I can escape the trap of worrying. Amen!

41. Help me to set aside my worry about how I will perform during my first phone interview. Give me the confidence to relax, smile, and answer the questions to the best of my abilities. Amen!

42. God, if I thought about You being my employer, then maybe that would help take the pressure off. Help me be of service to the job interviewer, even if they don't hire me. Amen!

43. Thank you for giving me a way to pay attention to what I am doing with my job search plan. Give me the strength to take action each day, and then reward myself for doing what I said I would. Amen!

44. Thank you for giving me the ability to learn new things about how to get the Applicant Tracking System software to screen me in. Amen!

45. Thank you for giving me a mind to learn new things. Give me the patience and confidence to improve my LinkedIn profile. Amen!

46. Thank you for giving me the patience to sort through what opportunities will work for me and just ignore the rest. Amen!

47. Protect me from my busy mind, particularly when my mind says abusive things to me like I am no good. Help me strengthen my ability to say "SWITCH" and then develop strategies to compensate for managing those nasty thoughts. Amen!

48. Help me practice gratitude when I wake up and each evening before I go to bed at night. Amen!

49. Guide my actions to do what it takes to keep going. Give me the strength to keep going, even when I am not seeing results. Help me trust that momentum will pick up as long as I keep taking action. Amen!

"MAY IT BE SO!" CHIN UP, CHIN OUT AND GO!

Acknowledgments

For me, it all started with trusting that inner voice that said, "Write a book for discouraged job hunters." I was going through a divorce, and I wasn't exactly in any shape to be writing for people who were down. Yet I kept hearing, "Write it anyway." So I did. I choose to call that inner voice God, and am grateful for my Christian faith which provided me a way to listen and discern. I am grateful for divine nudges. Next, I am grateful to Kathryn Hallett who dealt out tough love yet also was a fierce advocate to me. Once the book was written, my first readers were Scott Shepherd and Kathryn Voskuil Their feedback to me was invaluable. I concluded that the book was not finished and wrote some more.

Then Nancy Gardner and David Wood gave me their insights. I wrote some more. Then I hired Lizbeth Tanz to really give the book a once over. That was painful, but it did make the book better. I want to thank Tom Boutaugh for his generous donation to cover some of the set-up costs. I want thank Katie Gounis, my illustrator who took my sketches and made them beautiful. She was also part of the initial book cover design.

I want to thank Cathy and Jack Davis, at Davis Creative who gave me the tools to move this book project forward. Once the book was completed, I am grateful to Kelly Fiala who gave me intergenerational insights that strengthened this book. I want to thank Ed Mass who praised my writing and showed me that I had something valuable to say. And I want to thank my children Solveigh and Kristofer who gave me both encouragement and technical support. As you know, the work of writing is much easier when surrounded by a community of support, and I am so grateful for the support I received. There are others I cannot thank publicly: the thousands of career clients who taught me much as I guided them.

About the Author

Shary Raske was born the fourth of six children in Northwestern Ohio. Her parents, John and Charlotte Scheub raised her to believe that getting a college education, serving God, and serving her community was of upmost importance. They modeled for her the qualities of loyalty, generosity, and the value of hard work. She also learned that assigning work by gender was less desirable than work by aptitude and ability. Her brothers did their own laundry and ironing — and they all took their turn doing the dishes; and Shary, with her brothers, took turns plowing and caring for the livestock.

While Shary will be forever grateful for those lessons, she knew at an early age she wanted to live where there were sidewalks. In her senior year, her high school consolidated with their arch rival. This challenging transition gave her a first-hand opportunity to learn that when mergers are done badly, everyone suffers unnecessarily. Her dedication to organizational change principles were birthed from that experience. Her work as a career advisor began while working in the nonprofit sector. Shary found herself in charge of a project representing low-income professionals eager to learn a better trade and generate a higher standard of living. Shary soon found herself working hand-in-hand with employers to determine their talent needs and simultaneously, was able to develop opportunities for low-income workers to fill those needs. She was very successful in changing the trajectory of under-developed lives and wanted to accomplish more!

Always immensely interested in business growth, how leaders make decisions, and how professionals learn, Shary moved to Saint Louis when her children were still small, taking a position as a career management consultant for a nationwide firm. This career change offered her opportunities to train corporate leaders on how to negotiate better, resolve conflict faster, influence others (without being a jerk), and help teams be nicer to each other — all while still achieving productivity goals.

Shary then founded her own business, Courageous Change Consulting, LLC specializing in career change for corporate leaders and professionals. As a writer, speaker and coach, Shary's perspective and philosophy has been influenced by several well-known contemporary thought leaders including, Jack Chapman (salary negotiation expert), Barbara Sher (success teams to get what you want), Robin Sheerer (confronting and overcoming barriers to success), and Ramit Sethi (emotional intelligence and business growth). Being a nature enthusiast and adventurer, Shary's influence goes well beyond the borders of the United States, opening her St. Louis home and hospitality to many citizens of the world. Her guests have traveled from South American, the Middle East, Asia, and Africa — creating a cultural exchange where each share and gain great insights about the world.

Shary's current geography is centered around both Virginia and Missouri where her four grandchildren live. And she is quite proud of her now adult children — two amazing people who are kind, intelligent, musical, smart, curious, creative and constantly finding better ways of doing things. Shary values those traits, too. www.CourageousChange.net

85395914R00122

Made in the USA
San Bernardino, CA
19 August 2018